350

WILD BIRDS

OF THE AMERICAS

TERENCE MICHAEL SHORTT

WILD BIRDS
OF THE AMERICAS

HOUGHTON MIFFLIN COMPANY, BOSTON 1977

This book is published in the United States by
Houghton Mifflin Company through special arrangement
with the publisher of origin, Pagurian Press Limited.

Cover painting of Redbreasted Merganser
by Terence Michael Shortt
Burntwood Island, Lake Athabaska, Alberta, June 1945

ISBN 0-395-25786-7

10 9 8 7 6 5 4 3 2 1

Printed and bound in Canada

for
Audrey

INTRODUCTION

Terence Michael Shortt may well have seen and sketched from life more species of the world's birds than any other person alive today. I say this in all sincerity, and not without giving the matter a good deal of thought. Born on March 1, 1911 in Winnipeg, Manitoba, he has managed to visit during the twenty-four thousand or so days of his life every province of Canada, including islands of the high arctic; many parts of the the continental United States, as well as Alaska and Hawaii; Mexico, Trinidad, and Tobago; Colombia, Peru, Ecuador, and the Galápagos Islands; southern India, the Himalayas, Burma, Thailand, and Japan; Uganda, Kenya, and Tanzania; and, most recently, Madagascar and the Seychelles.

The point of the above paragraph, which reads like a gazetteer, is not that this remarkable man has visited all these places, but that he has looked for birds wherever he has gone, has found them, and has made action sketches of them. He has not been casual about this. As a rule he has known about what to expect at a given place, for he has consulted the proper books in advance.

Sketches present birds not as creatures of beauty primarily, but as organisms that are going somewhere or doing something. They illustrate and to some extent interpret action. A blurred photograph tells us clearly enough that wings have moved. A sketch of those same wings anticipates the stages of downthrust and represents the actuality of propulsion in such a way as to suggest the movement as a whole rather than a split-second part of it. The viewer's imagination supplies what the sketch does not show. This enforced participation of the viewer may, indeed, be that which gives the sketch a vigor that the blurred photograph does not have.

During most of his life, Terry Shortt has been obliged to crowd bird portraiture into his busy days as a museum man. Professionally he has been responsible for dioramas, temporary exhibits, labels, educational programs, and the like. Bird delineation has been his avocation. Aware of the special power that direct-from-life sketches have, he has made them partly as a guide for his finished work. His paintings have, therefore, that which demands participation of the viewer—participation as well as mere looking. How fortunate for us all that on his thirty-some expeditions to far-away places he managed to go ahead with his sketching undaunted by mosquitos, black flies, no-see-ums, deerflies, tsetses, ticks, leeches, jungle rot, frostbite, seasickness, and, I daresay, occasional spells of lassitude. Having made many direct-from-life sketches myself under what may be called, collectively, untoward circumstance, I know what it takes to make them.

This book is the first of a series of carefully planned volumes to be not only illustrated but written by Terence Shortt. Both paintings and words are a powerful plea for the preservation of the birds and of their habitat. Every person who looks at these pictures will find himself admiring, then . . . participating.

GEORGE MIKSCH SUTTON
Stovall Museum of Science and History
University of Oklahoma

CONTENTS

FOREWORD

When I was a small boy my mother arranged to have Aunt Ella give me piano lessons. Every week for one whole, long Manitoba winter I made the trip right across Winnipeg from Deer Lodge to Elmwood to maltreat the instrument. Then one spring day, long-suffering Aunt Ella phoned Mother and said, "I would advise you to encourage Terence with his bird painting." Dear Aunt Ella.

Some fifty years later and still adventuresome, I allowed myself to be dragooned into turning my hand to writing; indeed I nudged a manuscript past a succession of unfortunate and bewildered editors and into book form. My regret, in retrospect, is that Aunt Ella was no longer around to admonish me to stick to my painting.

Sapience comes late to some people. It is my hope that, since in this book I have allowed brush and pen rather than typewriter to show how I see birds and feel about them, here is an augury that at long last it is coming to me.

Even before I left school, I was captivated by the diversity of form and the color of birds. The more I saw of them the more I realized that the integral character of the face of each species relied on subtle patterns of feather arrangement and coloration and texture of unfeathered parts, as much as on the more obvious features; and the more determined I became to learn about them and to record their images.

This obsession, which fortunately remained a hobby and therefore never languished, has stayed with me all my life. As recently as 1963, when on a museum expedition, I collected a specimen of the jungle crow of India and wrote in my journal:

"... once again impressed by the individuality of the different species of *Corvus*. This one is a small, hyperkinetic raven, yet it differs manifestly from big *Corvus corax* in the curious conformation of the feathering of the forehead, crown, and nape ... am convinced that if one could achieve sufficient familiarity that every avian species could be shown to have distinctive nuances above and beyond those used in keys and field guides. ... "

What is it that gives a bird's face its character? It is often contended that personality, be it in bird, dog, or human is conveyed by the eyes. Yet an eye, as such, is merely an expressionless eyeball, capable only of involuntary dilation and contraction of the pupil in response to light. The expression in an eye is governed by the mobility of its surrounds of eyelids and orbital skin and their integumentary outgrowths — eyelashes, eyebrows, and other hair or feather appendages — and is largely a peculiarity of mammals and birds. (A rattlesnake's eyes do not change their aspect even when it strikes.) So it is, then, that our eyes change expression through the knitting of brows, crinkling of the surrounding skin, or varying of the aperture between the lids. It is essentially the same with birds. "Knitting of the brows" can raise a crest or the semblance of one and can reveal the emotions of anger, alarm, or curiosity. In some species (such as vireos and helmet shrikes) these feelings are eloquently expressed by lifting and ruffling the throat feathers. We can convey our feelings through the nose (flaring of the nostrils) and the mouth. The bill of a bird is nose and mouth in one, and, in the great majority of species, serves also as the hand — the tool of prehension. In a few species it probes and even feels (woodcocks, for example). It assumes the functions of lips and teeth: pulling, cutting, crushing, tearing, and grinding. It chips away and casts aside cover in the form of bark, gravel, or foliage that might conceal food. It is an organ essential to the prime functions of the bird and is modified to permit the occupation of many behavioral niches. But it has little latitude of expression. A few groups of birds with a flexible leathery area about the nostrils can flare them to a degree. The hard horny edges of the mouth are capable only of opening and closing, yet when opened can show, in conjunction with other features, aggression, fury, fear, or even affection.

The color reproductions in this book are *studies* made in the field, mostly from freshly obtained specimens, though some were painted directly from living models. The black and whites are translations of field sketches, the latter being to all but me indecipherable scribbles resembling the memo-pad doodling one sees by the telephone. Added to the field sketches that indicate posture at rest or in flight is the knowledge of anatomy and pterylography gained from preparing many specimens for the Royal Ontario Museum. The black and white drawings represent, in effect, the result of editing and interpreting raw materials. They were done in the studio with reference to sketches, notes, photographs, and specimens.

While I have always attempted to make my color portraits scientifically correct, I gradually learned that the essentials of avian features were more than just accurate diagrams drawn with the aid of calipers, and it became my first concern to try to capture the unique psyche of each kind. It must be admitted that all fall short of the artistry of reality. One comes up against the statics of paper, brush, and pigments; the inadequacies of eye and hand; and, in the field, the exigencies of the occasion: biting insects, cold, heat, rain, poor light, or the pressure of time, for there was always much other work to be done.

It should be said that if one depended for knowledge only on one's experience, one would not progress very far in bird study. One would have ignored the anatomies of Coues, Schufeldt, and Ridgway; the keys of Hellmayr and Witherby; the field guides of Peterson and Williams. So I would like to acknowledge my indebtedness to all these and many, many more. And, also to those wildlife artists who have through their artwork and writings provided insight and inspiration, among them personal friends — George M. Sutton, Allan Brooks, Lee Jaques, Roger Peterson, Don Eckelberry, and Shelley Logier. There are others known to me only by their works — Louis Fuertes, Leo-Paul Robert, Bruno Liljefors, Archibald Thorburn, Ernest Thompson-Seton, R. B. Talbot-Kelly, John James Audubon, and Elizabeth Gwillim. At one stage or another of my life, each of them (and others) has exerted a powerful influence on my way of seeing and thinking about birds and art.

My feelings about art have remained simple. To me depiction is essentially a form of sharing. The act of drawing, painting, or sculpting simply expands one's capacity to share. I feel that enjoyment of life is sadly marred without the communion of others. In my view, it is as simple as that.

I think, too, about early mentors — Bert Cartwright, Charles Broley, Alex Lawrence, Lester Snyder, Percy Taverner, J. H. Fleming, and Hoyes Lloyd for kindly interest and expert tuition to a callow young birder, and of LeMoine Fitzgerald, Roy Fisher, Fred Varley, Richard Wilcox, and Russ Hyder for both direct and inspirational instruction in what form and color are all about. So there are many people, besides my editors and myself, who have had an unseen hand in the preparation of this book. I hope I have not let them down.

14

1 Family *Gaviidae*
LOONS

Red-throated loon

Most books about New World birds have dealt with those species occurring in North America only, and it has become traditional to begin with the loons as the most primitive of our avifauna. For a number of reasons, it has been found expedient to do the same here, although some Neotropical groups are considered by most authorities as still more "primitive" — a term that poses many questions with few sensible answers. To those who feel inclined to quarrel with the arrangement of families herein, let me quote Dr. Elliot Coues, in my opinion perhaps the greatest of American ornithologists, who wrote in his monumental *Key to North American Birds* as follows: "... it must be obvious . . . that no linear arrangement of the groups can possibly exhibit their various interrelations; and consequently, any sequence of the families we adopt becomes a choice of evils."

The natatorial design in birds reaches its finest evolvement in the loons. The legs are perfect swimming devices — the most efficient paddles ever developed. In this connection it should be remarked that a bird's legs, unlike ours, are not separate from the body from the hip downward, but for a distance — that varies in different families — are enclosed within the skin of the body. In the loons this distance reaches to the "ankle." The foot, known as the "tarsus," is laterally compressed to a knife-blade configuration and flares out into long, wide-webbed toes. This wide paddle, securely anchored against the body, gives tremendous propulsive thrust; while on the return stroke the thin-boned toes fold into a narrow bundle which in concert with the knife-like foot slice back through the water with a minimum of resistance.

Loons are noted for their competence as divers and can swim long distances under water. They share with the grebes the ability to alter their specific gravity at will by inhaling or exhaling, so that they can sink down effortlessly into the water without diving.

Marvellously adapted for life in the water, they are cumbersome on land. The inability to bring the feet far forward (as, for example, in geese) prohibits a horizontal position of the body axis. They rest upright or nearly so, the whole foot is applied to the ground; progression on land is awkward and constrained, usually with a shuffling motion half on the belly.

Common loon ▶

Common Loon
Gavia immer

Loons are powerful fliers, progressing with strong, shallow, deliberate wingbeats, but because their bones are solid rather than pneumatic as in most other birds, the act of becoming airborne from the water surface is accomplished only after considerable effort and a long taxiing run.

There are four species of loons, all of them of northern distribution; indeed three nesting only in arctic regions. All but the small red-throated loon are essentially black and white. The latter differs in being more slender and in the introduction of soft greys and chestnut into its color pattern. All adult loons possess peculiarly shaped feathers on the neck, throat, or chest. These feathers have a white inwardly curving surface with raised black edges, which are distinctively firm, smooth, and polished — these patches can be *felt* as well as seen (The Loon's Necklace).

The best known, the common loon, is a bird of the rock-rimmed lakes in spruce and pine country, the vacation land of so many people. Its unworldly, melancholy cry with a quality of bittersweet sadness epitomises wilderness and is among the best loved of bird voices to those who have learned to enjoy unspoiled nature. In recent years its numbers have been reduced because chemical pollution of their food fishes causing eggshell thinning and non-hatching of young; because of too many summer cottages on their lakes, denying them the privacy they require for nesting; and because their nests are swamped (with the resultant floating out of the eggs) by the wash from high speed powerboats. On many of our northern lakes the morning and evening melody of the loon is now but a nostalgic memory.

2 PENGUINS

Family *Spheniscidae*

Penguins are so different from other birds that one eminent systematist proposed they be elevated to a subclass, separating them from the rest. Absence of flight feathers (found in all other living birds even if degenerate and useless, as in ostriches and emus) was one of his criteria; but evidence of the existence of embryonic quills shows that their long-ago ancestors were probably flying birds.

Nonetheless, the wing of a penguin is quite unlike that of other birds. It has evolved into an efficient, seal-like flipper. It is uniformly covered by tiny, scale-like feathers; indeed, penguins' bodies are also completely clothed, the feathers are not in separate tracts with broad naked spaces in between — as in most other birds. (Check this with your Thanksgiving turkey!) The feet are fat and fleshy and, like loons, the legs are housed to the ankle in body skin. Unlike loons, they are able to walk on land, albeit in a human-like vertical posture and with a fat man's waddle.

Penguins — some fifteen species — are all birds of the southern hemisphere, although not necessarily, as is often stated of Antarctica; in fact, only two nest south of the Antarctic Circle and several kinds are subtropical, with one, the Galápagos penguin, qualifying as tropical—its home range is almost on the equator. It would appear that this species reached such lofty northern latitudes because of the cold Humboldt Current which sweeps the Galápagos Islands.

It is often incorrectly stated that owls are the only birds with binocular vision. Many other groups — herons, loons, grebes, cormorants, boobies, and mergansers have binocular vision when looking forward and *downward*. Why? Because of

TmShort

Galápagos Penguin
Isla Fernandina, Galápagos
May 1965

the narrowness of the lower portions of the head — chin and cheeks — and the mobility of the eyeballs. These birds need this mobility because of their pursuit of prey beneath them in the water. Such is also the case with penguins.

Galápagos penguin braying

The name "penguin" is a misnomer for it was originally applied to the great auk. It seems to have stemmed from the Welsh *pen gwyn*, "a white head" (possibly because of the great white oval patch on the face, or from the unknown winter plumage), as this was the name given to it by early seamen.

◀ *Galápagos penguin*

3 TINAMOUS

Family *Tinamidae*

If the voice of the loon expresses the mood and spirit of our north country in summer, then the melancholy cadences of tinamous embody the great lonely dimness of a variety of tropical and subtropical habitats from Mexico to the pampas. Their mournful yet soothing whistles, in descending or ascending series, are given by both sexes, usually only at dawn and twilight.

There are about fifty species of tinamous which, in the well-known abhorrence nature has to a vacuum, take the place of other fowl-like birds — pheasants, grouse, quail, francolins, and guinea fowl — over much of the Neotropical and the southern temperate regions of South America.

Though superficially they resemble bobtailed partridges, they are a distinct family, regarded by some authorities as the most primitive of living birds (whatever that means). Although they have well-developed pectoral muscles, their flight is feeble, of short duration, and almost uncontrolled, possibly because of their tiny hearts and inadequate lungs. Tinamous are cryptically colored in woody shades of brown, buff, and warm grey — as befits their surroundings of dead leaves on the forest floor, sere grasses on the pampas, or the ground litter of thickets.

The shells of tinamou eggs have a glaze that suggests the finish on a piece of fine French-polished furniture. They come in a surprisingly un-egg-like range of colors, from turquoise through to the rich red-purple of wine. Usually only one is laid in a mere scrape among the leaves or other debris on the ground, and, since polyandry is the rule in tinamou society, the male incubates the eggs and raises the chicks. There is a predominance of males — perhaps four to one — and it is the hens who conduct the courtship rituals and do most of the "singing," often frenziedly, while the cock, possibly recalling his last long stint of domesticity, reacts with philosophical restraint. Although there must be considerable rivalry among hens for the few available males (when most are already sitting on eggs or caring for chicks), the absence of spurs on their legs (such as on cock pheasants and tom turkeys) and their reliance on vocal inducements suggest that the blandishments are carried out in a ladylike fashion.

Little tinamou

4 GREBES

Family *Podicepedidae*

In 1790, Latham, in designating a title for the grebes, intended to translate the old English name of "rump-foots" into Latin. This would have, appropriately, given them the appellation of *Podice-ped-idae*, with the added charm of wit. But with less than flawless mastery of Latin grammar, Latham performed an etymological head-over-heels and the word came out as *Podi-cepit-idae* — the "rump-heads"!

For a long time this name had to stand, as it was against the canons of zoological nomenclature to correct an error. But recent, more sensible amendments have been made and the malapropism at last has been stood on its feet.

Grebes resemble loons in many anatomical details; for example, the legs are housed largely within the body skin (the reason for the mistake detailed above), but differ from them conspicuously in that the toes are not connected by webs. Rather, each toe is equipped with a series of lateral lobes or flanges so hinged that the lobes flare out on the propulsive swimming push and automatically fold around the toe on the return stroke, thereby greatly reducing the area of water resistance.

The tail feathers are soft and downy, stick up jauntily, and give the bird an impression of being a big overgrown chick.

The plumage of the breast and belly is extraordinarily dense, waterproof, and satiny. It was found so attractive by nineteenth century exponents of high fashion that breast pelts were used for muffs, capes, hats, and evening bags. In the

Pied-bill grebe ▶

24

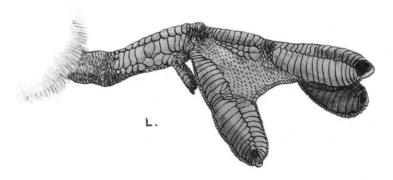

L.

Pied-billed Grebe
Pimm, Swan River, manitoba.   Aug. 12, 1935

TMShort

trade they were known as "grebe fur." Grebes were killed by the thousand. At one time pelts sold in the Eastern markets for twenty cents a breast.

Courtship antics of the Western grebe

This is a remarkable family: many species have highly decorative crests, manes, and ruffs; their irises are often brilliantly colored, many with different shades of bright red with a white or silvery ring around the black pupil; they have a habit of swallowing their own feathers — apparently as roughage and even feed them to their young. Most singular are their courtship displays — both male and female participate, with an astonishing degree of synchronization. The best known and perhaps the most spectacular (certainly the most readily observed for it is performed on the prairie lakes) is the courtship display of the Western grebe. This species has several clearly demarcated love dances, in one of which the mating pair rise up side by side and, with necks curved gracefully forward and down, race across the water in a nearly vertical position.

5 Family *Diomedeidae*
ALBATROSSES

To oceangoing sailors albatrosses and wind are synonymous. Superstitious seamen of old lived in awe of the "bird that brings the wind." Their conviction was immortalized in the poem by William Taylor Coleridge, "The Ancient Mariner," in which the overzealous killer of an albatross was made to wear it around his neck in punishment and atonement. One wonders if the great wings were tethered up or allowed to dangle free; if the latter, then the penance was severe indeed!

Like most superstitions and old wives' tales, there is truth behind the association of the albatross and wind; for if water is the element of a duck, and a tree the element of a perching bird, then wind is the element of the albatross. Without wind the bird is virtually grounded; with wind it is the master of gliding flight. The mistake in the sailors' reasoning was, of course, that it was the wind that brought the albatross and not the other way around.

Four of the thirteen species occur in the northern hemisphere. The others never cross the equator; their range is as circumscribed as that of sheep enclosed by a sheep fence — the unseen barrier is the hiatus of wind in the windless doldrums that occurs around the equator in both Atlantic and Pacific Oceans. Albatrosses abound in the Roaring Forties and the Furious Fifties where powerful west to east winds blow almost without cessation.

The stiff, narrow wings of albatrosses are extremely long, especially in the upper arm and forearm. Each wing has from forty to fifty flight feathers. Unequalled power for soaring flight is conferred upon them by such an airfoil. Albatrosses can follow a swift-moving cruise ship for days on end, circling it, veering off, and returning to cross and recross its bows with hardly ever a detectable wingbeat.

Waved albatross

In bygone days, human comfort posed a threat to the continued existence of albatrosses. The great sea birds were killed by the thousand at nesting colonies so that their feathers (sold as swan's-down!) could be used for stuffing pillows and mattresses. Today, their only adversary, strangely enough, is the airplane—not because the airplane can outmanoeuvre them (for it can't) but because man requires the albatrosses' island nesting grounds for airstrips. The birds have such territorial constancy that they will not and cannot be made to move.

Black-footed albatross ▶

28

Blackfooted Albatross ♀
Diomedea nigripes
Gulf of Alaska, Sept 8 1936

6 Family *Procellariidae*
SHEARWATERS

Found on all the seas and oceans of the world, shearwaters are great migrators. Some of the fifty or more species probably travel farther in a year than any other living creature. They spend most of their lives on the wing and the distances covered are immense.

The name "shearwater" for these seabirds is a fitting one, for they skim low over the water along the troughs of giant waves, and sweep up over the crests almost effortlessly. When the sea is becalmed, shearwaters resort to a flapping power flight and so are more resourceful than the wind-dependent albatrosses. Even in the power flight their characteristic mode of progression is by a few rapid wingbeats and a gliding sail on rigid wings.

When feeding the shearwaters literally do walk upon the water, an endowment often wrongly attributed to the storm petrels, which just *appear* to. Without entirely folding their wings, shearwaters land on the water surface with their feet and, balancing with their airfoils, "walk" forward over the water as they pick up food from near the surface.

Some species are known as whalebirds. In the old days they were used by whalers as indicators to show the presence of whales; rightly so because they are inordinately fond of krill, small crustaceans, which are the favorite food of the right whale. It follows that where there are krill, there will likely be both shearwaters and whales.

A peculiarity of pelagic (sea) birds, which this group shares with the albatrosses, is that they secrete large quantities

30

of oil from special glands lining the proventriculus (the digestive portion of the stomach). The oil has several uses: one, it is used defensively — regurgitated with accuracy and force at an adversary (or a supposed one!); two, it is fed to the young; three, it is discharged through the nostrils and spread over the

Greater shearwater

feathers for dressing plumage. It may also have some function in conjunction with the salt-excretion glands which lie within the skull and are necessary to rid the birds, through nasal-drip, of excessive sea salt. Sea salt can become highly toxic and even lethal. The oil gives the birds a singularly unpleasant smell of frowsty musk with an innuendo of iodine. Cabinets containing museum specimens of seabirds reek of this oil, even though the housed skins may be several decades old.

31

7 Family *Hydrobatidae*
STORM PETRELS

Were it not for the twenty-odd species of birds in the storm petrel family, it might be presumed that the attributes of the albatrosses and shearwaters were prerequisites to bird life on the open ocean, especially on the stormy southern seas. Yet the storm petrels are small birds slightly resembling slender, long-legged doves. They have a fluttery flight that is the direct antithesis of the rigid glide of the big birds of the southern seas.

Never rising far above the water surface, storm petrels skitter about erratically — feet dangling, hovering, staying, and spurting — like gadflies over a pool. They are active twenty-four hours a day.

Seamen of old thought petrels walked upon the water, as the apostle Peter is said to have done (with debatable success), and so called them "little Peters." It is from this colloquialism that they get their name. But their hanging toes seldom touch the water, and it is probable that their dancing feet serve to gauge distance — a mere touch of an uprising swell alerts them to lift clear.

Another superstition has them as omens of disaster, and in this connection they are known as "Mother Carey's chickens." Since Mother Carey was the seafarers' nickname for the Virgin Mary (from *Mater cara*, the divine guardian of sailors) the relationship is not clear, unless the presence of storm petrels was taken to augur shipwreck and a near-at-hand departure for heaven.

Storm petrels feed largely on zooplankton, the abundant,

wandering, drifting, tiny animals that live in the upper layers of the oceans and which with the plant forms, phytoplankton, are the basic food of all the other creatures of the sea. Rough water disturbs plankton making it accessible, hence the association of storms and storm petrels. In calmer weather petrels follow ships; the ships' wash and wake stir up and bring to the surface this manna of the sea.

Galápagos petrel

Storm petrels excavate long, deep burrows; a remarkable exploit for creatures with long, slender, weak bills and small, delicate feet. The nest, placed in a chamber at the end of the burrow, is visited only during the night.

8 Family *Phaëthontidae*
TROPIC-BIRDS

Red-billed tropic-bird

Tropic-birds are the bos'n birds of the seafaring men of old. A fancied resemblance between the long streamers on the birds' central tail feathers and a marlinspike account for the name. In this age of jet aircraft it may be necessary to elucidate: a bos'n (boatswain) was a ship's officer who, first, was responsible for the sails and rigging, and, second, had to rouse the men and summon them to duty. This meant mobilizing the men at any hour of the day or night to hoist, shorten, or strike the sails as the winds freshened, shifted, or died. A marlinspike was a pointed iron or hardwood tool used by the bos'n for separating strands of rope in splicing. But it was also used on the heads of recalcitrant sailors during the discharge of the bos'n's second responsibility. Hence the acute awareness of the crew to anything even remotely resembling the bos'n's marlinspike.

There are three very similar species of tropic-birds. For most of the year they roam the open oceans of the warmer parts of the world, their only companions the albatrosses, shearwaters, and storm petrels. Many people only glimpse a tropic-bird when one or two approach and circle a ship at sea. Unlike most other seabirds, they soon lose interest in the "moving island" and maunder away.

Their flight is graceful and tern-like but with more rapid, regular, and deliberate wing-beats, and when they dive for their fishy prey their descent is more restrained and less flamboyant than the terns' dashing plunge. Often they will drop in a slight, steered spiral.

Instant identification of the tropic-birds is provided by their long streamer-like tail feathers (which project a foot beyond the tail) and a bold black-and-white wing pattern.

Tropic-birds nest in natural cavities and ledges on rocky cliffs or steep slopes, usually not far from water but sometimes far inland. To those who know them only as seafaring birds it comes as a surprise to see their brilliant snowy-white forms drifting across a mountain slope against a backdrop of the lush vegetation of the tropical rain forest.

Like many of our most gorgeous land birds, the *Phaëthontidae* have sacrificed vocal accomplishment for physical beauty. To my knowledge their only utterance is a strident, squealing "pickit-pickit-pickit."

Red-billed tropic-bird ▶

Redbilled Tropicbird ♀
Phaethon aetherus

Tagus Cove, Galápagos
May 1965 -

American White Pelican
Pelecanus erythrorhynchos

Johnston Lake
30 mi. South of Moose Jaw.
Saskatchewan

June, 1954.

9 Family *Pelecanidae*
PELICANS

To comment on the bill of the pelican is almost banal; nevertheless we shall do so, hoping to present more information besides its capacity to "hold more than its belican." The bill is several times as long as the bird's head. It is slender but straight, strong and flattened, and ends in a claw-like hook. On the underside the mandibular rami (singular *ramus*, Latin for a branch) which are extensions of the lower jawbones and are fused together for most of their anterior length in ordinary birds, in the pelican join only near the extreme tip of the bill and are capable of moving apart several inches while remaining hinged at the tip. Between these rami hangs the pouch, an immense three-layered skin bag—on the outside, the skin; on the inside, the mucous membrane; and, in between, a thin layer of two sets of slender muscular fibres running in opposite directions. By means of the rami mechanism, the pouch can be contracted so as to either occupy little space, or, it can be expanded into a huge pendulous bag.

The pouch or gular sac extends down to include the throat — indeed in the brown pelican, it stretches half way down the neck and, when extended, has the capacity to hold more than a

◀ *American white pelican*

American white pelicans, flock-feeding

gallon of food and water. (The much larger white pelican's pouch can accommodate three gallons!)

It was once thought that pelicans used the pouch to convey live fish, swimming in fresh water, to the young. In fact, after making a catch with its dip-net, the pelican closes and elevates its bill, contracts the pouch (which forces the water to run out of the corners of its mouth), and then swallows the fish. The young are fed on macerated, half-digested fish which are regurgitated into the throat and pouch and dribbled into the youngsters' mouths. When older the chicks stick their short-beaked heads right into the throat of the adult who is retching at the same time. It is like a wrestling match, and the writhing and contorting are both alarming and revolting.

The brown pelican is an air-to-water diver, plunging straight down in a bent-wing dive from as much as thirty feet in the air. It hits the water with a splash and sometimes even submerges. The American white pelican is a communal fisher. A flock first locates a school of fish from the air. The pelicans alight and form a line or crescent with the fish between them and shallow water. Then, like a well-drilled company, they advance with flapping wings and much splashing, driving the fish before them. When the fish reach the shallows, the carnage takes place.

10 Family *Sulidae*
BOOBIES and GANNETS

The members of this family are particularly interesting for the bird portraitist. Although all seven species are more-or-less of a size, similar in general conformation, and with little variety in their plumage colors (white, black, grey, and brown), each has an eye-catchingly distinctive face. Though all have long, stout bills, bare faces, and small gular pouches, these parts exhibit an exquisite range of coloration, from palest green, grey-blue, slate, blue-black, yellowish-pink to red and orange-yellow. The eyes, also, range from near white through pale blue and yellow to grey-brown.

In addition, there *are* subtle differences in bill shape, contour, and symmetry. The lineation of the naked spaces, too, is tenuously distinctive — all in all a challenging project for the painter, for the aggregate of small physical differences makes large character differences.

Boobies are strictly marine birds, powerful and streamlined. All have heavy bodies and long, narrow wings of great strength and sweep. These characteristics, combined with air-sac shock absorbers under the skin, make them pre-eminent as air-to-water divers. Frequently they plunge from great heights on to their finny prey and at such times are completely immersed, often swimming after and catching the fish if they failed to grasp it on the first contact.

Boobies are among the most thrilling of all birds to watch, particularly when a flock of several hundred have found a large school of fish. They rain down — often a dozen or more in free

Blue-footed booby ▶

40

Immature

Blue footed Booby. ad ♂
Sula nebouxii
Isla Fernandina, Galápagos.
May, 1965.

fall at once — while others, their quarry taken, circle upward for another dive.

Yet, they suffer the maligning appellation of booby, "a silly dull-witted fool, a lout." Why? Because the guileless birds often alighted on the deck or rigging of ships and allowed themselves, unresisting, to be picked up and added to the ship's larder. The implication is that any animal that is not terrified of man is stupid, reasoning that perhaps cannot be denied, but a sorry indictment of the disposition of the human race.

Red-footed booby

In a more cheerful vein, let us conclude this account with the observation that gannets have no brood patches, and those races that lay but a single egg incubate it by spreading their big, webbed, splay feet over the egg after first having warmed their feet in the sun!

11 Family *Phalacrocoracidae* CORMORANTS

The name of this family comes from the Greek and means "bald ravens" — perhaps an allusion to their colorful naked faces, for none is bald in the modern sense and many have the crown or nape adorned with a stylish *panache*.

Cormorants are aquatic birds of the seacoasts and larger freshwater lakes of all but the high arctic regions. They feed on fish which they capture by diving from a swimming position on the surface. Like pelicans, tropic-birds, and boobies, cormorants have all four toes joined by webs. They are efficient underwater swimmers and dive to great depths, but their wing feathers are not waterproof and after a fishing excursion they perch with wings outspread to dry — like washing on a line. Even the flightless cormorant of the Galápagos dehydrates its pitiful little pinions in this manner. Nature, it would seem, slipped up here.

Cormorants are colony nesters. Some communities are immense — Peruvian cormorant or guanay colonies number in the hundreds of thousands, and their excrement (guano) at one time covered some islands off Peru and Chile like a great lens with a depth of more than fifty meters at its focus! When the birds from these huge colonies are out fishing, the whole sea and sky are filled with them.

Today guano is collected as fertilizer for human agrarian use. Because of its high nitrogen content, it is more than thirty-three times as effective as barnyard manure, and the guanay has been called the most valuable bird in the world (to the human economy). We dispute this, remembering the red

Guanay

jungle fowl of Asia, the progenitor of all domestic chickens. When we consider the value of the chicken and its egg in the markets and supermarkets of the world and how much both contribute to the human food supply, the stinking powder of the guanay birds, valuable as it is, fades into insignificance.

Flightless cormorant ▶

M Short

A Gigantic Cormorant !
Pupil elliptical, the vertical axis longer.

Flightless Cormorant
Nannopterum harrisi
Isla Fernandina, Galápagos
May 1965.

12 Family *Anhingidae* SNAKEBIRDS

Variously called snakebirds, water turkeys, darters, or anhingas, these birds are the original underwater spear fishermen.

In the systematists' jargon they are closely related to the cormorants but have one significant anatomical difference — the curious conformation and articulation of the neck vertebrae. The neck vertebrae also have tiny eyelets through which the tendons pass. The result is a strong crook in the neck, similar to that of herons, and designed for the same purpose: to give the bird the ability to thrust its head forward powerfully and quickly and, conversely, pull it back.

The snakebird is a strange looking bird, with its body, wings, and feet resembling a cormorant's but with a long sinuous neck and a small constricted head that tapers directly into the very acute, straight, and slender beak. It is, then, like a slender cormorant with the neck and head of a heron.

Snakebirds are found mostly in the warmer regions on the quiet waters of lagoons or on willow-margined shady ponds. They perch easily and dive from a swimming position with amazing celerity. Often they swim with the body submerged and with only the head and long snake-like neck showing. (Hence, snakebird and *anhinga*, the latter a Brazilian Indian name with the same interpretation.)

Snakebirds take their food (fish) underwater: a forward thrust of the head, propelled by the ingenious neck mechanism, stabs the fish (even armour-scaled gar) and impales it on one of the dagger-like mandibles, usually the lower one. The fish is then lifted out of the water, juggled around to a headfirst alignment, and swallowed whole. Generally in this gulping process the bird's body remains immersed, and on these occasions the serpentine resemblance is great indeed.

Because of their ability to alight easily and take off from tree limbs, snakebirds build bulky nests in branches, often placed among the nests of other species, in a heronry, for example.

On fine days a flock of anhingas will indulge themselves in a kind of aerial dalliance. They mount high in the sky, sailing with the ease of buzzard hawks. Their long slender necks, wings, and tails give them the appearance of flying plus (+) signs. They circle upward, crisscrossing each other until almost out of sight, then, one bird after another folds its wings and plummets down with spine-tingling speed.

Anhinga

13 FRIGATEBIRDS

Family *Fregatidae*

Frigatebirds, or, as they are sometimes called, man-o-war birds (in Spanish, *rabihorcados*, forked rumps) are an anomaly. They are strictly pelagic birds that don't go in the water.

Although they look big, frigates weigh little more than three pounds, yet have a wingspan of about eight feet. Proportionately, they have the largest wings of any bird. In flight they seem to be all wings. An American white pelican or a Peruvian brown pelican with an equal wingspread weighs in the neighborhood of forty pounds! In addition to the slightness of the body, the feet are exceedingly small and the legs extraordinarily short.

The immense length and sweep of the wings and long, forked tail give them a command of flight that is unsurpassed. They delight in soaring to astonishing heights — often actually rising out of reach of strong binoculars. But they cannot dive, and can barely swim or walk. They get their piscine food from the sea by dashing down and snatching it from the surface with unerring aim, causing hardly a ripple. It is a treat to watch them plucking just airborne flying fishes on the wing, literally off the snouts of pursuing porpoises and tuna.

The piratic English name comes from their habit of harassing cormorants, boobies, pelicans, and other hardworking fishers until they drop or disgorge the fish they have just caught (and they are not above using roughhouse tactics on those slow to comply). With a magnificent swoop, the frigate invariably intercepts and retrieves the falling fish

Magnificent frigatebird ▶

Magnificent Frigate Bird ♂
Fregata magnificens
Off Albemarle I. Galápagos
April 1965

before it reaches the water. They are truly avian freebooters; their facility for picking food from the water or out of the air is aided by the long slender bill which is equipped with a powerfully hooked nail — an efficient single-clawed grapnel.

Like their nearest relatives, the cormorants and snakebirds, frigatebirds have a gular sac; but in the frigates that of the male has the elasticity to inflate into an extraordinarily enormous brilliant red balloon. (Everything about frigates seems to be extraordinary!) This throat pouch evidently serves some function as a sex-recognition feature.

Frigates nest in colonies. Their rough stick platforms are placed in low trees, usually mangroves lining a shore. A frigate community is a busy place, or appears so, for most gestures are accompanied by the flick of a wing — a four-foot flick!

Lesser frigatebird

14 Family *Ardeidae*
HERONS

Most people have seen a great blue heron standing in statuesque immobility or stalking with single-minded deliberation in the shallow waters of a lake or in a quiet back eddy. But most people call it a blue crane!

The herons, all sixty-three kinds, have long, dagger-like beaks which they use for spearing their prey — fish, frogs, and other aquatic animals. The space between the beak and the eyes is unfeathered and the beak seems to run directly back into the eyes; actually it opens just beneath them.

Herons have loose plumage emblazoned with greatly lengthened feathers. The feathers form beautiful crests and elegant chest and back plumes and ornament many forms during the breeding season, reaching their finest form in the magnificent train of diaphanous feathers which rise from the shoulders and spread far beyond the tail of the snowy egret.

The term "egret" is simply a corruption of the French word *aigrette*, a heron's plume. Aigrette has been adopted into English to mean a tuft of feathers or fur or a spray of gems. The name "egret" is usually, but not invariably, given to white herons but its application is purely conventional and has no more classificatory meaning than "pigeon" and "dove."

The largest of the American herons is also the best known — the great blue heron which stands between four and five feet tall. It is easily distinguished from a crane by a heron family peculiarity of the cervical or neck vertebrae. These vertebrae are of unequal length and the neck tendons pass through disparate apertures in the vertebrae in such a

Galápagos heron

way as to produce a decided flex or kink, thus enabling the heron to fold its neck back when flying until the head seems to rest on the shoulders — the bird-watchers' field-mark for herons. It also provides a sort of taut bow-string tension on the neck tendons when the heron's neck is cocked in fishing, and a "pull of the trigger" sends the head and dagger-like bill flashing forward to impale its prey with the rapidity of a rattlesnake's strike.

At the other size extreme is the little least bittern, no more than a foot long and an inhabitant of the cattail marshes; but the tiny bird has all of the same characteristics as its big cousin. The bitterns are wonderful examples of concealing coloration, and the markings of the least make it extremely difficult to detect among the cattails. Its concealment is enhanced by its habit of standing rigid with bill pointing skyward, presenting to the suspected enemy only the striped underparts which simulate the vertical stalks around it. Meanwhile, its extraordinarily mobile eyes are directed downward in their sockets and peer out, past the throat, straight at the intruder.

Great blue heron ▶

Great Blue Heron ♂
Ardea herodias
Minesing Swamp, Ont.
May 1958.

T M Shortt

15 BOAT-BILLED HERON

I shall never forget my first sighting of a boat-billed heron. I was collecting in the Caroni Swamp in west Trinidad one evening, when a large bird that I took to be a black-crowned night heron flew into view. Perfunctorily, I swung my binoculars on to it, and, just as I brought it into focus, it yawned. Merciful heaven, a flying bullfrog!

This cousin of the herons has a beak so unlike the spears of other herons that it is usually placed in a family by itself. But even more significant from the evolutionary standpoint is the presence of an extra pair of "powder-down" tracts. These tracts are curious mats of down feathers, remarkable in that they continue to grow indefinitely. Because of this unlimited growth, there is a continual breaking up of the ends, which causes the patches to be dusted over with a dry, scurfy exfoliation. This has an unpleasant greasy feel like powdered graphite. The function, if any, of these strange tracts is not clearly understood, but it is thought that the powder may be used in dressing the rest of the bird's feathers. The tracts occur in such diverse groups as hawks, parrots, gallinaceous birds, the cuckoo-roller of Madagascar, the frogmouths of Australia, and herons — birds of such unrelated families and of such disparate habits and habitats that no clue can be found in this direction. In the true herons there are six mats positioned in pairs: two on the lower belly under the hips, two on the lower back over the hips, and two on the breast. The boat-bill's fourth pair lies on the shoulder blades. It has powder puffs at the ready for any emergency.

54

Why a bird with all the features of a heron should need such a bizarre beak is a puzzler. The beak is like an inverted flour scoop equipped with a lid and a steel trap hinge. It may be more effective for picking up frogs and lizards than a spear, or it may be that it is useful in gripping the smooth shells of crabs, which the boat-bill also eats.

Like night herons, boat-bills are crepuscular in hunting, and therefore have enormous eyeballs — generally almost black although some that I observed were dark red. Certainly the eye-shine reflected from a torch beam was red.

Boat-bills have a very long, wide crest which is not often noticed as it is seldom erected other than in courtship display. At other times it lies flat on the shoulders and reaches halfway down the bird's back.

Boat-billed heron

16 STORKS

Family *Ciconiidae*

Storks are essentially birds of the Old World, where there are upwards of a dozen kinds including the well-known white stork renowned in fable and myth (and idle talk!). There are three species in the New World, only one of which occurs in North America. This is the American wood stork which, until recently, because of its strongly *downcurved* beak, labored under the unfortunate and confusing name of wood "ibis." It still carries the ludicrous generic name of *Mycteria* ("I turn up the nose"), a title originally bestowed on the great South American jabiru, a bird with an immensely large, recurved bill. Thus, a bird with a downcurved beak is labelled as having an upturned one. The world of taxonomy is indeed out of Alice in Wonderland, a house of distorting mirrors.

Wood storks breed from South Carolina, the Gulf Coast, and the Gulf of California, south to Argentina and Peru. They frequent the most thickly wooded swamps and bayous. They fly by alternately flapping and sailing, and, like all storks (with the exception of the adjutants and marabous), with legs and neck fully extended. At times they mount high in the air and perform the most beautiful evolutions, with the wings motionless. The wood stork has a number of colloquial names, all of which are more piquant than its official name. Among these are "flinthead" and "gourdhead," depictive of the bird's bare head and neck which are rugose and scaly. The bare head is crowned by a horny plate. Storks feed in the shallow water and coastal flats at low tide and will consume almost any kind of animal matter, from largish fish and crabs to insects.

American wood stork ▶

56

Wood Stork ♂
Mycteria americana
Río Cordoba, Mexico
Aug 1946.

T.M.Shortt

The Maguari stork, or *Baguari*, resembles the conventional stork as exemplified by the common European white stork, but it is at once recognizable by a blaze of brilliant scarlet skin around the cold, staring white eye.

Wood stork

The jabiru is a gigantic, entirely white stork with a bare head and neck. The neck is thick and goiterish looking, black like the head but with a broad bright red collar around the lower portion. The huge bill is straight along its upper border, curving upwards toward the tip. The lower mandible arches sharply upward. The lineation of the beak opening and the mouth also are upcurved, giving the bird the appearance of being possessed with waggish good humor. Jabirus may be seen striding unmolested among the people in some Indian villages in tropical South America. Almost the size of adult humans and larger than children, they look curiously human as bird and man pass each other without so much as a glance, like two pedestrians on a busy city street. The storks' value as scavengers and rat exterminators is recognized; in turn the birds find the litter and filth of the village good hunting ground.

17 Family *Threskiornithidae*
IBISES and SPOONBILLS

White-faced glossy ibis

Ibises and spoonbills are medium-sized, stork-like birds. They differ from storks in that the covering of the bill for most of its length is soft and leathery rather than hard and horny.

The family divides into two groups which are distinguished by the shape of the bill. The ibis group has long, thin, strongly downcurved bills like those of the curlews. In fact, one American species was formerly called the "Spanish curlew." The spoonbill group, as the name implies, has the tip of the bill dorso-ventrally flattened into a wide spatula-like end.

Historically ibises and spoonbills have had mixed treatment at the hands of man. At one end of the scale was the deification of the sacred ibis as the god Thoth by the people of ancient Egypt. The birds were even mummified by the same process used for mummifying the pharaohs—placed in beautifully crafted sarcophagi of the size and in the likeness of the bird, then buried in the temples along with the pharaohs.

At the other end of the scale was the shocking massacre of hundreds of thousands of white ibises and roseate spoonbills (along with egrets) in the United States in the nineteenth century, when their feathers were greatly valued by the millinery trade.

Fortunately, the birds have survived both extremes, as well as many others in between. And how the wheel turns! The rare Japanese ibis, a white bird with a red face, has been declared — not a deity — but a national treasure by the Government of Japan, in an effort to protect the one small remaining colony.

More benign attention has been given them by the artists of the world. Ibises have captured the imagination of sculptors, carvers, and painters back to the wall paintings of early Egypt, a millenium before the birth of Christ. They were a favorite subject of Japanese and of Chinese painters from the Sung period (*ca*. 1200 A.D.) to the nineteenth century. Grace and symmetry of form, tranquility of stance, simplicity of color and pattern — even their reflection in quiet water — made them frequently chosen subjects for the delicate yet bold style of Far Eastern artists. Today they are avidly sought as subjects for color-film photography.

A colony of ibises and spoonbills is a busy place. The birds are forever coming and going, bringing new sticks, or stealing sticks from other nests and quarreling over them. Feeding of the young is a vigorous process, for their food is a semi-digested pablum of regurgitated crayfish, snails, small snakes, frogs, slugs, and bugs. The chick sticks its head into the maw of the old one, who retches until the moppet is satisfied.

Roseate spoonbill ▶

60

Roseate Spoonbill ad ♂
Ajaia ajaja
Caroni Swamp. Trinidad
May 1957

T.M.Short

(mangroves)

(?)Immature with feathered head

18 Family *Anhimidae* SCREAMERS

The screamer has long been a thorn in the side of those concerned with the orderly linear classification of birds. Consider first that its affinities, based on internal characteristics, dictate that it should be placed in the order *Anseriformes* along with the familiar ducks, geese, and swans. Then observe that the screamer's beak is constructed like that of a pheasant or a grouse; that its feet are proportionately gigantic with the long toes virtually unwebbed and supplied with long, strong claws; that its feathers grow uniformly all over its body rather than with bare spaces between tracts as in the waterfowl; that it lacks uncinate processes (a series of splint bones proceeding obliquely from each rib to shingle over the next succeeding one and increasing the stability of the bird's "side-walls," found in all other birds except the fossil *Archaeopteryx*, the oldest known bird, that lived in the Upper Jurassic 140,000,000 years ago); that it possesses two large sharp spurs on the forward edge of each wing at the "wrist"; that when (as it frequently does) it indulges in soaring flight, it most resembles a broad-winged eagle; that it has developed pneumaticity to a greater degree than any other bird — the bones, even the tail-bones, the toes, and the tips of the wing-bones, are hollow and are connected to a system of air-sacs between the muscle and skin, a condition otherwise associated with pelicans; that it inflates for vocalizing — the startling two-syllabled, trumpet-like scream is preceded by a rasping, crackling sound caused by the filling of the air-sacs in the manner of a human inflating his lungs prior to a great shout.

None of which dilutes our admiration for the ebullient, turkey-sized birds of the marshes, wet grasslands, and forest lagoons of South America. But it sometimes suffers a reversal when screamers interfere with our surreptitious stalking of less vigilant swampland birds.

Screamers fly up, often to the top of a dead, drowned tree, and sound an alarm which can be heard for more than a mile. Their song is almost incessant, particularly during the night.

Of the three species, the best known is the crested screamer or *chaja* (cha-ha), the latter name native onomatopeia derived from its cry. It takes well to captivity and is often exhibited in zoos where it has been known to breed.

Crested screamer

19 FLAMINGOS

Family *Phoenicopteridae*

There is little need to describe the appearance of flamingos. They are the familiar and decorative attractions in zoological gardens and resorts. The beauty of the much publicized flock that inhabits the infield at the Hialeah Race Track in Florida is said to help assuage the smart of losing bettors. Suffice to say that with their long spindly legs and equally long gracefully curving necks, they are the giraffes of the bird world.

But there are other interesting things about flamingos. The most remarkable is the unique shape of the bill and its method of employment. It bends abruptly in the middle and its edges are furnished with many oblique laminae or "strainers." Beyond the bend the upper mandible is nearly flat. When feeding, the head hangs down at the end of the long neck and is upside down, with the lower mandible on top and the flat upper mandible below. To illustrate how the bill works, let your arm hang limply and place the terminal two knuckles of your fingers on a flat surface. Now, move them slowly from side to side in a sweeping motion. In flamingos, of course, the bill is opening and closing on the minute aquatic life in the water — tiny molluscs and shrimps, small worms, insects, algae, and other near microscopic living things — and the tongue is pumping against the roof of the bill to drain off the water through the strainers, which prevent the ejection of food particles.

Three species of flamingos occur in the New World. The greater flamingo is the best known. In a different color phase

Greater flamingo ▶

64

(white and rosy instead of carmine) it also lives in tropical and warm temperate regions of the Old World. It is the best known and supplies most of the exhibition birds, including the race track flock mentioned above. Its range includes (or included) the Bahamas, parts of northern tropical America, and the Galápagos Islands. It also occurs as a paler, more pinkish bird in temperate South America from Peru to Chile and Argentina. Some authorities consider this a distinct species: the Chilean flamingo. Two more small species, the Andean flamingo and the James's flamingo, have restricted ranges in the lakes of the Andean highlands.

Courtship display of greater flamingos

Flamingos have long strong wings which are quite adequate for their small bodies, but which appear small and deficient against their great length as they fly with long, drawn-out neck and beanpole legs fully extended. They often form long lines, crescents, and chevrons when travelling any distance and are noisy both in flight and while feeding. Their vocalizing is strongly reminiscent of geese — a loud honking and a conversational gabble characteristic of feeding flocks.

20 Family *Anatidae*
DUCKS, GEESE, and SWANS

Since time immemorial waterfowl have won man's favor more than any other bird group. Pintails, geese, and other waterfowl are depicted with scientific accuracy and unaffected artistry on the walls of the temples of ancient Egypt, and they appear in the art of all the great civilizations since. They have inspired poetry and music — *Le Cygne* by Camille Saint-Säens and *Ein Schwan* by Edvard Grieg are two examples.

Also, since time immemorial ducks, geese, and swans have been favored as edibles and are the quarry in one of man's favorite sports. That they have survived all this adoration — for there is much truth in the old proverb that man "destroyeth that which he loves" — is a tribute to their wariness, powers of flight, fecundity, and adaptability. Countless tons of lead shot have been flung at them and in North America alone over a hundred million acres of their wetland breeding grounds have been drained for agriculture. It is to man's credit that in recent years he has restored upwards of five million acres of ponds and marshes as waterfowl refuges. Combined with sensible hunting regulations, this would seem to ensure the existence of satisfactory numbers of most species (and satisfactory numbers for the table) for many years to come.

Waterfowl have been divided into three simple groups by laymen as far back as history has records — the ducks, the geese, and the swans. That these nonprofessional classifications largely stand up to the onslaughts of the experts is gratifying; we should always remember that the

Canada goose ▶

Canada Goose
Branta canadensis

Canvasback ♂
Nyroca valisineria

Big Point Channel, Athabaska Delta
Alberta.
June 10, 1945

fundamental mission of nomenclature is to insure that you know what I am talking about and vice versa, whether the object of discussion be a particular kind of bird, a chair, or Ann Smith. Changes in language should be made only after conscientious deliberation.

Whistling swan rising from water

Even among the hot blooded, amorous class *Aves*, waterfowl are salacious to a remarkable degree. The production of hybrids is frequent, with intercrossing between swans and geese, between diving ducks and mergansers, between pond ducks and eiders, and many other improbable combinations. Pintail x mallard and mallard x black duck are the most common in the wild state. The frequency of occurrence of half-breeds between the latter pair and the fertility of their offspring hint that they might well be considered conspecific. On the other hand, the prevalence of sterility among other hybrids as well as other factors, such as unbalanced sex ratios and the unlikely eventuality of two like fertile hybrids meeting in the wild, effectively prevent their perpetuation.

Members of the family occur wherever there is water, from Tierra del Fuego and the Falkland Islands to the edge of the permanent arctic ice pack.

◄ *Canvasback*

21 Family *Cathartidae*
NEW WORLD VULTURES

We think of vultures as birds with the revolting habit of eating dead and decaying flesh. But in many tropical towns and villages and indeed in the countryside they are recognized for what they are. Those who gave them their scientific generic names were also aware of their usefulness and called the turkey vulture *Cathartes*, a purifier, and the black vulture *Catharista*, I purify. Those who look upon them with contempt might also disdain our city works departments which remove our refuse and keep our streets clean. And we should remember that it is we who make much of the revolting mess that they get rid of. Garbage dumps in Port-of-Spain and Guayaquil are kept sweeter than are many such disposal areas in temperate regions thanks to the great numbers of volunteer purifiers.

The American vultures must wait for carcasses to decay before feeding upon them because their beaks lack the tearing ability of eagles' or the larger hawks' beaks.

There are six species of American vultures. The most familiar is the turkey vulture which ranges north to southern Canada, and the black vulture, the common bird of more tropical regions. Rarer are the two giants, the California condor and the Andean condor, and the eagle-sized, strikingly colored king vulture. The sixth is the lesser yellow-headed or savanna vulture, a bird closely resembling the turkey vulture except that the naked head is yellow and bluish rather than red. The flamboyant yellow, orange, red, and bluish head of the king vulture, along with those of the ocellated turkey of Central America and the two ground hornbills of Africa constitute the

71

most outlandish bird faces that I have ever painted. They very nearly outstep the boundaries of credibility.

Vultures detect their food with keen eyesight and not, as the mistaken notion persists, by smell. This was proven more than six hundred years ago by Emperor Friederich II of Hohenstaufen who conducted experiments and wrote in his book *The Art of Hunting with Birds* (the first truly great bird book), that they found their food by eyesight alone. The truth is that the olfactory organs of nearly all birds are poorly developed—perhaps a good thing for the vultures who must subsist on such a malodorous diet.

Andean condor

Bacteria, including those that carry human diseases, pass through the digestive systems of most animals in a still viable state. Not so with those that enter vultures; the vultures' potent juices effectively kill all. We shall never know how many epidemics have been prevented by these "loathsome scavengers."

King vulture ▶

72

Sarcorhamphus papa
King Vulture
Yaguachi Marshes, Ecuador

Tom Shortt

22 AMERICAN QUAILS

Family *Phasianidae*; subfamily *Odontophorinae*

No true pheasant is indigenous to the New World although several have been introduced by man. One, the ring-necked pheasant, has flourished in its new home and is one of the few alien species whose permanent naturalization is not open to question. Others are the European starling, the house sparrow, and the rock dove. The rock dove is better known as the domestic pigeon.

Members of the subfamily of American quails are easily distinguished from the grouse, the other gallinaceous birds of the New World. They are considerably smaller, with short inconspicuous tails (except in the tropical wood partridge group), the legs are naked rather than feathered, the nostrils are shielded by a naked scale rather than a dense mat of small feathers, and many have crests of remarkable shape.

Where grouse are birds of the forests and plains and even the tundra and alpine-arctic northern regions, quails prefer warmer climes. The familiar bobwhite reaches north to extreme southern Ontario but most other species are tropical or subtropical in distribution. Several kinds inhabit the deserts. Quails also differ from grouse in being quite vocal (many of the sounds made by grouse are mechanical). The calls of quails are often described as "songs" for they are usually melodious whistles, whinnying trills, or other pleasant musical sounds.

Pleasing characteristics of this group are their handsomely patterned plumage and the presence in many species of chic stylish topknots and chignons. The mountain quail has an arrow-like crest of two slender, keeled plumes three to four inches in length which stand straight up. The California quail and the desert quail have elegantly recurved crests of six or more keeled, club-like, glossy black imbricated feathers more than an inch long. The elegant quail of Mexico has a similar one which is made up of several feathers graduated in length from front to back with the rearmost the longest, only slightly recurved, and of a gorgeous shade of tawny yellow. The scaled quail has a short, full, soft crest of snowy white. The banded quail has a straight, slender black crest tipped with rufous and inclining backward. The spotted wood-quail's full, lush crest is orange. Strangest of all is the crest of the Montezuma quail which hangs behind its head like hair bundled up in a snood but which, when the bird is alarmed, spreads out laterally until it more than half-encircles the head and looks like a mushroom.

Long-tailed wood partridge

The quails have suffered heavy hunting pressure, but their proliferation, their wariness, and their speed both afoot and in flight have ensured their survival. The more recent threat — decimation of their habitat — is much more serious.

23 Family *Accipitridae*
HAWKS and EAGLES

The name "hawk" was originally applied to the goshawk and the Eurasian sparrowhawk and was derived from the Dutch *havik* and the German *habicht* probably from the root *haf*, to seize. Applied to American forms this more discriminating interpretation would restrict the use of the name to the goshawk, Cooper's hawk, sharp-shinned hawk, and a number of Neotropical species: the bicolored, Gundlach's, tiny, semicollared, and grey-bellied, and possibly the savanna hawk.

Unfortunately, the name has been used imperceptively for birds that should properly be called "buzzards" (Swainson's, red-tailed, red-shouldered hawks, etc.) and "harriers" (marsh hawk). These misnomers, however, are now so firmly rooted that correction would impair the usefulness of decades of literature and cause more confusion than now exists. Thus are the sins of the fathers visited upon the children.

Accipitridae, a very large family, embraces more than two hundred distinct species. In the Americas it includes, in addition to the hawks, buzzards, and harriers named above, the eagles, eagle-hawks, and kites. Collectively they are diurnal birds of prey, in the main killing for themselves and disdaining refuse. They are lumped together by "... anatomical features of a highly technical nature."

Because a number of species prey on waterfowl, grouse, and other "desirable" birds (meaning ones *we* want to eat) they have been regarded by man as competitors; when a few

Bald eagle ▶

76

Bald Eagle
Haliaeetus leucocephalus

found barnyard fowl handy and non-elusive quarry, the whole
family acquired a bad name and many innocent mouse and
gopher eaters were slaughtered. Even today some States have
as yet to extend legal protection to these important elements in
the general ecology of things.

Hawks and eagles are renowned as birds of noble, if
savage, countenance. Their fierce expression originates in the
possession of a pronounced, horny superciliary shield (a
glowering "eyebrow") often in conjunction with glaring red or
cold yellow eyes.

Mating flight of red-shouldered hawk

24 Family *Pandionidae*
OSPREY

Although another species is known in fossil form from western Europe, the osprey is the lone surviving member of its family. It is one of the widest ranging of all birds, occurring throughout the northern hemisphere excepting only the arctic regions. It is also found in Africa, the East Indies, and Australia, but strangely enough it has never penetrated South America.

An osprey's plumage is close and firm, the feathers overlap like tight-fitting tiles or scales and are oily, having an unpleasant, almost befouled greasy feel. The feet are immensely large and strong and covered with rough granular scales and spiny tubercles. All toes are free to their bases (without trace of webbing), with the outer one versatile. That is, it can be pointed forward or swung backward like a second hind toe. The claws are very large and, unlike those of hawks and owls, of equal length and greatly curved. Instead of being scooped out on the undersurface, they are subcylindrical. All these peculiarities are in evident adaptation to their semi-aquatic, piscivorous habits which demand a waterproof plumage, great wood-rasp-like toes and grappling-hook talons to grasp their slippery quarry.

A fishing osprey is a thrilling sight. It cruises in circles at heights up to seventy yards until it spies a fish near the surface. Then it plunges in a bent-wing dive, at a speed that causes an audible rushing sound of air passing around and between the great stiff flight feathers. At almost the last moment, the long legs are flung forward, and the taloned feet extend in front of the head. After the resounding splash (the

Osprey ♂
(*Pandion h. carolinensis*)
Eleanor Cove
Yakutat Bay, Alask
May 29, 1936.

TMShortt

bird often being completely immersed) it rises, shaking the water from its plumage (like a dog or a cat) and, after rearranging the fish to a head forward position, flies off to its perch or nest to eat it. During the period of raising the young the male does most of the fishing, bringing his catches to the female who feeds them to the nestlings.

Ospreys build enormous nests of sticks, some so thick and long that one wonders how they transported them. The nests are usually high in a giant dead tree, but occasionally on the ground. The nest is added to, layer by layer, year after year, for up to twenty years until some are as large as a garage.

Although its builders resemble eagles or large hawks, small birds are not fooled and often, finding the big nests to be deluxe thickets, build *their* nests within them.

◀ *Osprey*

25 Family *Cracidae*
CURASSOWS and GUANS

This group of about forty species is peculiar to the more
tropical regions of the Americas; one species, the plain
chachalaca, penetrates into the United States to the lower Rio
Grande Valley of Texas. *Cracidae* belong to the large order of
gallinaceous birds commonly known as fowls, which include
the pheasants and quails, grouse, turkeys, and guinea fowl.
But they differ from most of their relatives in being essentially
arboreal and most species live in the gloomy depths of the
great, humid tropical forests.

The best known is the plain chachalaca, a common species
of the tall brush and thickets of eastern Mexico. It makes its
presence known by its loud, raucous voice which often drowns
out those familiar sounds of the tropical dawn — the crowing
of cocks and the barking of dogs. A group of thirty or more,
each outdoing the other with strident shouts of "cha-cha-lac"
produces one of the most absurdly comical of all bird
vocalizations — a sound of wild revelry.

The curassows of the genus *Crax* are stately birds. They are
of the size of turkeys; the males are black with the underparts
and tip of the long tail white, curly, feathered crests, and a
large, round, fleshy, yellow knob at the base of the bill. The
smaller hens are bright rufous with checkered black-and-white
crests. Like other members of the *Cracidae*, they run nimbly
along branches high in the forest canopy like squirrels or tree
iguanas. When they fly it is for short distances, with an
awkward flapping of the rather short but deeply rounded
wings and fluttering glides. They make strange muffled

amphoric calls — their curious ventriloquial quality is amplified by air cavities in the neck.

Another turkey-sized member of the family of bizarre appearance is the horned guan, now restricted to the humid forests of a few volcanic peaks in extreme southeastern Mexico and southern Guatemala. It has a thick, erect, bright red "horn" on the crown, whose brilliance is intensified by the contrast of the velvety black feathers of the head.

Great curassow

26 Family *Falconidae*
FALCONS and CARACARAS

The falcons and the caracaras are included in a single family because of certain skeletal characteristics of the bones of the shoulder-girdle and of the skull which are different from those of other diurnal birds of prey. Thus, inwardly related, the two branches of the family have diverged widely in outward appearance because they have pursued different ways of life.

The falcons exhibit raptorial nature in its highest degree. They are birds of medium or small size (the pygmy falcon of Africa and falconets of Asia are but the size of sparrows), sturdy build, and a vigorous, fiery disposition. They pursue living prey which they capture, often in flight, by violent onslaught. The caracaras are more vulture-like, chiefly terrestrial, and subsist largely on carrion.

Perhaps no group of birds has been so universally admired as the true falcons. A falcon (probably the lanner falcon) was deified by the ancient Egyptians as the god Horus. Falcons have been trained to hunt for man's food and for sport as early as 2000 B.C. in Central Asia and possibly as early or earlier in the Far East. The use of falcons for hunting dates back at least 1400 years in Europe where edicts stated what classes of people could use which raptorial birds.

One of the earliest, truly splendid paintings of birds, worthy of a twentieth century master, is of a peregrine falcon poised on the wrist of a young falconer, rendered by the Dutch artist, Aelbert Cuyp (1620-1691). It is probably the first bird painting in which the feather systems are handled with understanding.

Peregrine falcon ▶

shallow
wing stroke

Peregrine Falcon ad ♂
(Falco peregrinus anatum)
Fort Ross, Somerset I. N.W.T.
September 1, 1938.

In post-nuptial moult. - replacement shown in new buff breast
feathers, blue back & c.

Prairie falcon

The wings of the true falcons are ideally designed for swift sustained pursuit. They are long and pointed and the flight feathers are rigid and tapered. Along with certain swifts, they are conceded to be the fastest flyers in the animal kingdom; some experiments indicating speeds up to and possibly exceeding a hundred miles per hour in the final dive or "stoop" on flying quarry.

While the distribution of falcons is world-wide — from the cold regions of both hemispheres to the tropics—the caracaras are restricted to the warm temperate and tropical regions of the Americas. Caracaras' wings are long but lack the compact hardness of those of the falcons and their flight is heavy and raven-like. They seldom soar, and they engage in aerial gymnastics only in the courting season. Convergent evolution has given them the vulturine features of a naked face and weak feet with little-curved claws unsuited for seizing strong living prey.

27 Family *Tetraonidae*
GROUSE

Tetraonidae are strictly a north temperate zone family; in the New World no species reaches south into Mexico. It is a small compact group with a readily recognized character, yet within the family kinship there is sufficient modification due to conditions of environment and behavior that the seventeen world species must be divided into no fewer than eleven genera, each with distinctive adaptive features. Five of the ten North American species are the only living representatives of their genera. The other five are the three ptarmigan of the genus *Lagopus* and the two prairie chickens of the genus *Tympanuchus*.

All grouse have the nostrils covered by a mat of feathers; a naked strip of skin above the eye developed into a "comb," and the feathering of the legs extending well on to the tarsus (in the ptarmigan right to the ends of the toes). Some kinds have evolved horny, fringe-like pectinations on the toes in winter, a sort of snowshoe adaptation. There are nearly as many kinds of tails as there are genera. Some have curiously modified feathers on the neck which may be umbrella-like as in the ruffed grouse, or stiff and wing-like as in the prairie chicken.

The sharp-tailed and blue grouse and the prairie chickens have large, inflatable sacs on the neck, the naked skin of which is highly colored — orange in the greater prairie chicken, pinkish in the lesser prairie chicken, yellow or plum-colored in different geographic races of the blue grouse, and purplish-blue in the sharp-tail.

Pinnated grouse

Several species have remarkable courtship performances. They gather in traditional dancing grounds called "leks." Here, the males adopt highly ritualized postures, issue strange booming, cooing, gobbling, and cackling sounds, and engage in mock combat. The precise function of these communal displays is not clear but they seem to promote a general social stimulation prior to mating.

Ptarmigan are unique in the family in undergoing a seasonal color change — all three species adopt a nearly all-white winter dress. Birds of high boreal or alpine distribution, ptarmigan have some seasonal movement to lower latitudes or altitudes. These "migrations" are accomplished on foot! The "p" in ptarmigan has been the butt of much humor (pterrible ptempered ptarmigan, for example) and perhaps rightly so for the name comes from the Gaelic *tarmachan*, a mountaineer (it has nothing to do with termagant!) so the "p" is spurious and was probably affixed by some pretender to erudition in classical Greek.

Willow ptarmigan ▶

Willow Ptarmigan ♂ & ♀
Lagopus lagopus
Cape Henrietta Maria
James bay, Ont.
July 3, 1948.

28 Family *Meleagrididae*
TURKEYS

The name "turkey" for the two species of this New World game bird family is another of those unfortunate malapropisms that are all too common in zoological nomenclature. The name was originally adjectival, "turkey cock" and "turkey hen," and was applied in Europe through the misconception that the imported fowl had originated in Turkey. The main progenitor of all the Thanksgiving and Christmas main courses was the Mexican race of the wild turkey. It had been domesticated by the peoples of southern Mexico long before the arrival of Christopher Columbus. Stock was introduced into Spain in the early years of the sixteenth century.

Its appearance in England dates from one served to King Henry VIII. That renowned trencherman must have found it toothsome because for some years afterward all turkeys raised in England were reserved for the royal table. But by the latter part of the sixteenth century the birds were being reared in great numbers and it is said that the Pilgrim Fathers brought descendants of the early Mexican stock with them on the *Mayflower* in 1620, perhaps unaware that the northern form of wild turkey was then abundant in the woods around Plymouth, Massachusetts.

When it was realized that the northern birds were larger than the Mexican birds, they were introduced into the domestic stock in an effort to increase the size of table birds. It is ironical that today, with pressures on income and the trend to smaller families, turkey breeders now strive to produce a *smaller* (ten to fifteen-pound) turkey.

The second species of turkey is the ocellated turkey. It is a smaller, highly iridescent species with peacock-like spots on its tail coverts and tail feathers. It has not been domesticated. Its naked head is one of the most bizarre in the whole wondrous heterogeneity of bird faces — a brilliant blue (changing in hue and shade with emotion, even as the common turkey can become flushed to blushing red) dotted with round and oval caruncles the size of peas in shades ranging from off-white through yellow and tawny to vermilion.

Turkeys have been an annual source of embarrassment to me. In spite of, or perhaps because of, having dissected thousands of birds with scalpel and forceps in the course of my work, I still make a mess of carving the festive bird before an expectant audience.

Wild turkey

29 Family *Gruidae*
CRANES

There exist about fourteen species of cranes, most of which inhabit various parts of the Old World. Only two kinds, the whooping crane and the sandhill crane occur in North America and none has ever occupied any part of South America. All are large birds; some of immense stature, standing five feet tall. The whooping crane is the tallest of all North American birds and probably even exceeds the standing height of the big flightless rheas of South America.

The most singular feature of cranes is one that doesn't show outwardly — the astonishing length of the trachea or windpipe. In the whooping crane the trachea is as long as the bird itself; fifty-five inches or more, with about half of it coiled away within the sternum or breastbone which is "excavated" or hollowed out to receive its remarkable convolutions. Within the sternum it forms several coils, folding back and forth around each other before emerging to pass on to the lungs. This design is probably responsible for their unrivaled sonorous, resonant trumpetings with vibrant overtones that can be heard several miles away. In our other species there is a difference but merely in degree, not in kind, as only about six to eight inches of the trachea enters the breastbone and its total length is little more than two feet.

In North America there has been much confusion of identity between cranes and the larger herons and, oddly enough, between cranes and turkeys. The great blue heron is erroneously called "crane" or "blue crane" by the majority of

Sandhill crane ▶

Sandhill Crane ♂
Grus canadensis canadensis
nr Hay River, Gt Slave Lake NWT
June 1959 -

TMShortt

people who see it standing in the water near their summer cottage. In the West the sandhill crane was almost universally known as "wild turkey" probably because of its large size and the naked red patch on the head (its flesh is quite as tasty).

Whooping crane

The whooping crane, teetering on the verge of extinction since the beginning of this century, exists in pitifully small numbers. The publicity given to the efforts of the governments of the United States and Canada, and of the National Audubon Society and other conservation agencies to ensure its survival has made it the most newsworthy bird in the world. Whether or not the unflagging exertions of those associated with its preservation prove successful, they have succeeded in capturing public sympathy to an unprecedented degree. The cause of the conservation of wildlife generally cannot fail to benefit from this arousal of public interest.

30 Family *Aramidae*
LIMPKIN

Limpkin

Although anatomically crane-like, the limpkin's outward appearance and whole ecology are those of a large rail. It is the sole member of its family and ranges from southern Georgia, Florida, and some of the West Indies south to central Ecuador and Argentina. It owes its English name to its hesitant, halting gait, but it is anything but disabled and is capable of a fine burst of scurrying speed when it has to. It also perches readily in trees and runs sure-footedly along the branches.

TonShnH.

Aramus vociferus ♂ Limpkin. Tamiami Trail Fla 1962

The limpkin's wailing cries are discordant, far-reaching, and nearly impossible to describe adequately, although they may be said to resemble human wails or howls. The crying starts at sundown and can continue all through the hours of darkness. As a result, the limpkin has many colloquial names: crying-bird, clucking-hen, courliri, wailing-bird, courlan, carau.

They are competent swimmers but weak flyers. When flying they carry the wings at a curiously high angle in relation to the body; a high-winged flight that is probably unique. They feed to a large extent on freshwater snails which they bring ashore before extracting the meat and leaving the empty shells. Accumulations of shells along muddy shores are good intimations of the presence of limpkins.

Seldom seen except in early morning or late evening, limpkins seem to be the disembodied spirits of lonely marshes and bayous. Their furtive, watchful appearance along the edges of densely vegetated waterways on a misty cockcrow has a ghostly insinuation that can have an imaginative person glancing uneasily over his shoulder.

◀ *Limpkin*

31 Family *Heliornithidae*
FINFOOTS or SUNGREBES

Neither of the accepted English names for these thoroughly aquatic birds is appropriate. Sungrebe is a poor name, for they are unrelated to the true grebes and are, in fact, lovers of the shady margins of stagnant streams and rivers with densely wooded banks. They are usually seen (if at all!) under the forest undergrowth overhanging the water. They suffer their other name "finfoot" because the toes are laterally rimmed with lobes or flanges like those of grebes, coots, or phalaropes, but bear little resemblance to conventional fins, such as those of fishes.

They have elongated bodies, compact waterproof body plumage, and swim with the body mostly submerged and the long, stiff tail flat on the surface, giving them a superficial resemblance to cormorants. Although the wings are perfectly developed they are reluctant flyers and prefer to dive or take cover if disturbed by scrambling ashore and scurrying into the thick underbrush. Curiously, for birds of such watery habit, they possess neck and head plumage that is soft and almost downy.

The distribution of finfoots is puzzling. There are three species, one found from southern Mexico to Argentina; another inhabiting perennial rivers and streams with thickly wooded banks and also coastal creeks where there is thick mangrove cover in tropical Africa from the Congo to northern South Africa; and the third along similar jungle streams in Malaya and Sumatra. They would appear to be the last relics of a once wide-ranging family. Today they are nowhere plentiful, which, combined with their shy, secretive habits, has made it difficult to learn their life history.

Finfoots are known to build rough nests of sticks, reeds, and water vegetation on low horizontal limbs not far from the water's edge and they climb up to them. The young are

Sungrebe

covered with down and probably desert the nest soon after hatching and make their way to the water — like ducklings. The females are somewhat larger and more decisively patterned and colored than the males. It is also known that both sexes attend the eggs and the young.

32 Family *Rallidae*
RAILS, COOTS, and GALLINULES

This family comprises about 120 to 130 distinct species and divides into three fairly distinct groups: the rails, the coots, and the gallinules. In the New World the members of these subdivisions are easily recognized, one from the other, but when world forms are analyzed they are found to merge into each other so closely that no clear distinctions can be made.

All are inhabitants of marshes, swampy woods, or wet grasslands. All have strong legs, being particularly heavily muscled on the thigh and on the crus (the leg proper or "drumstick," often wrongly called the thigh), and all have long toes by means of which they are prevented from sinking in mire or floating vegetation. They have dumpy bodies, short soft tails, and rather inadequate, round concave wings. Although they fly weakly with dangling legs, paradoxically, some species undertake long migration flights.

The rails range from sparrow-size and smaller to chicken-size. Their bodies are blunt and deep at the rear with short perky upturned tails, taper almost to a point in front, and are more laterally compressed than most birds. Their physique enables them to thread their way easily through the closest growing reeds, rushes, and undergrowth. Their bodies, in fact, strikingly resemble in configuration those of fleas. And why not? After all, the physical *aspect* of their respective habitats is the same! They are also responsible for the expression "thin as a rail" which has nothing to do with fence rails or railway tracks. This subdivision of the *Rallidae* is often divided into two main groups: the rails proper with

American purple gallinule ▶

100

American Purple Gallinule ♂
Porphyrula martinica.
Cropiche Swamp, Trinidad
May 1957

moderately long, slender, slightly downcurved bills (Virginia, king, clapper, etc.) and the crakes with short, stout bills which are high and compressed at the base (sora, yellow, little black, etc.), but these two types are bridged by the wood rails and other tropical species so that the distinction is not significant.

King rail

Gallinules are much like enlarged short-billed rails but the body is not so compressed. Also, they have a frontal shield which is an extension and expansion of the upper portion of the bill on to the forehead as a kind of broad, bare, horny plate. The toes are slightly fringed and most kinds swim well.

The coots are duck-sized and the most adaptively aquatic of the family. Their bodies are slightly depressed rather than compressed, and the toes are furnished with wide, flat, scalloped edges.

Of all birds, members of this family are the most vulnerable to the onslaught of man — his domestic animals, his unwanted cohorts (rats, mice, etc.) and his marsh-draining proclivity. Historically, quite a few members of the *Rallidae* were flightless and many inhabited small oceanic islands. These have been the most indefensible and as many as a dozen and possibly more have been exterminated.

33 SUNBITTERN
Family *Eurypygidae*

Deep in the tropical rain forest, one stands in the semi-dark surrounded by a colonnade of the straight, distantly spaced trunks of giant trees, their great leafy canopy a hundred or more feet above. Each great bole appears to be one of the evenly arranged pillars holding up a solid mass of roof twenty feet thick. None of the towering trees is deeply rooted and their massive, contorted substructures meander over the surface of the floor on which a thin layer of fallen leaves is rapidly being destroyed by multitudes of micro-organisms and fungi of endless variety.

It is a quiet place. The stillness may be sporadically broken by a sharp popping sound which echoes through the naves of the forest as a seed capsule of the sand-box tree explodes noisily and scatters its seeds in all directions. Or, perhaps a trogon intones its amphoric hooting call which seems to come from speakers hidden in the trees. Mosquitos hum and whine, and occasionally a big blundering beetle or a whirligig mantid, like a tiny helicopter, whirs across one's line of vision. An endless chain-belt of parasol ants, one line ascending, another descending a smooth-barked spiralling liana; each descending ant carrying an irregularly shaped piece of green leaf ten times its own size. Millions of pieces have to be transported by the army of bearers from the canopy to the underground nest where, fermenting, they become food for the fungus which the ants cultivate and, in turn, eat. Each round trip for a square inch of greenery means one of the little leaf-cutters must travel more than a hundred yards.

Now the forest becomes thicker, less easily penetrable. Roseau palms, their trunks encircled by close rings of vicious, three-inch thorns, appear. Here and there grows a tree-fern, ten feet tall with nodding six-foot fronds more than a yard across. The dead leaves on the ground become wet and treacherously slippery. Lianas are more abundant, some twisted, some oblate and ribboned, some look like ropes.

Sunbittern

Bird voices become more noticeable as the understorey grows denser, for we are now approaching the margin of a forest pond or sluggish stream. Shade and moisture-loving herbaceous plants and the natural seedlings of the great trees can grow here. Most of these ground plants have broad, tissue-thin leaves to promote photosynthesis, to profit as much as possible from the diffused light, and also to facilitate transpiration.

The margins of the pond are barely visible; they are overhung and overgrown by a rank growth. The waters are shadowed by the overreaching canopy edge and only dappled spots of sunlight hit the surface. The shores and banks are almost impenetrable, clothed in ferns, creepers, caladiums, and giant arums; most of the water's surface is covered by a mat of water lettuce, water hyacinths, and lily pads. The overhanging tree limbs and even the lianas, getting some sunlight, are festooned with epiphytes — ferns, bromeliads, orchids, and even arborescent cacti.

In the shallow water, almost invisible beneath the overhanging vegetation, is a medium-sized, somewhat heron-like bird. It is not tall, nor does it stand straight like a heron; it stalks along with its body near the horizontal but with the same kind of intense concentration as it gazes into the water. Then, like the strike of a rattlesnake, the head darts forward and a minnow is speared by the long thin bill. This is the sunbittern in its forest home.

It is a bird about sixteen inches long with a longish, thin neck and very full, broad wings and tail. Its plumage is soft and owl-like and its wings and tail are the most intricately, delicately, and gorgeously patterned of all birds. They are reminiscent of the mosaic-like designs of the great silk moths. The exquisite patterns are colored in black, rich yellow, chestnut, white, and dove grey.

The sunbittern often spreads its wings and tail when basking on a sunny perch. Sometimes the tail is shaken in a fantastic dance and the wings are drawn forward to encompass the head. At times it will freeze in this posture and the pose may be held for more than a minute.

34

Family *Jacanidae*
JAÇANAS

Jaçana should be pronounced zhá-saná for it comes to us through the Portuguese from the Tupi Indian name for the bird in Amazonia. If that is too difficult, say ja-cá-na — few will know the difference. It might have been easier if we had chosen to adopt the colloquial name used in India, lily-trotter, or the Australian name, lotus-bird.

By any name they are "queer birds" for they have the most overdeveloped toes in the whole avian repertoire. The New World species are only eight inches from bill-tip to the end of the tail, yet the middle toe and its long straight claw are a good two inches long and the other toes are almost equally as long. The straight claw of the hind toe is longer than the toe itself. Such a spread of toes enables the jaçana to run with ease over water hyacinths, water lettuce, lily pads, and other floating vegetation that so characteristically cover the pools, ponds, and old river courses of the tropics.

Jaçanas lift easily into the air, fly well, but present a strikingly different appearance from their relatives, the rails and plovers. Their wings are full, broad, and rounded towards the ends, and the flight feathers are a bright shade of greenish yellow. In addition, the long legs and toes trail behind, inclining slightly below the horizontal. They seem conscious of their garishly colored wings and on alighting, or frequently after running over lily pads, will pose with wings fully extended until they touch over the back.

Jaçanas build their nests on the unanchored mats of vegetation in lakes and sometimes strong winds will shift their floating island from one side of a lake to the other, carrying the nest with it. The nesting birds appear totally unconcerned; to jaçanas it matters not which side of the water to call home.

The Mexican jaçana has a curious frontal shield, an extension of the bill on to the forehead, which is three-clefted like a *fleur de lis* and is bright yellow. That of South American birds is bifid and red but their adornment also includes two long fleshy red wattles that hang down on either side of the gape. There are several well-marked geographic varieties in which the body color ranges from deep chestnut through maroon to black. There is also variation in the color of the frontal shield and wattles; in some birds these parts are bicolored red and yellow.

Northern or Mexican jaçana

35 OYSTERCATCHERS

Family *Haematopodidae*

It might have been more decorous to have called these seafood gourmets "oysteropeners" instead of oystercatchers for oysters do not run fast. Be that as it may, the bill of the oystercatchers, though clumsy-looking, is a marvellously efficient tool both for prying open the shells of bivalves and extracting the meaty oyster and for shearing off the adhesive stalks by which barnacles and limpets attach themselves to rocks.

The bill is straight and hard, longer than the head, much compressed (almost like a knife blade towards its end), and truncated like that of a woodpecker; in fact it resembles a coarse pileated or ivory-billed woodpecker's bill — except that it is bright scarlet or vermilion as if painted with gloss enamel. The bill, in some old individuals, is often worn thin and rounded from the constant abrasion to which it has been subjected over the years. Often these thin bills are warped sideways as if habitually used in one direction, perhaps suggesting left or right "handedness."

The family name, roughly translated, means blood-footed, often misinterpreted to imply red-footed for nothing could be further from the truth. The big, pale, fleshy feet, with only three toes, look as if they have become swollen and leached white from long immersion in water. The feet do, however, have an abundant blood supply and bleed freely when cut, and this may have inspired the name.

Set off by the jet black plumage of the head, the eyes of oystercatchers seem exceedingly large and bright. The illusion

Black oystercatcher ▶

BLACK OYSTER-CATCHER ♂
(*Hæmatopus bachmanni*)
MAY 25, 1936
OSIER ISLAND
DISENCHANTMENT BAY
ALASKA.

is caused by the yellow brilliance of the irises, surrounded by thick, turgid, naked eyelids — flaring red. Oystercatchers on the European side of the Atlantic seaboard have red irises.

There are about half a dozen species of oystercatchers with almost world-wide distribution. Most of them are pied black and white; a few are uniformly sooty or slaty black.

Oystercatcher — Galápagos Islands form

A resting flock of a hundred or more, all facing one way on a surf-rimmed rocky shore, boldly black and white with their bills forming brilliant stabs of bright red, are a glorious sight. They are even more spectacular in flight, revealing the bold white lower back patch and black-tipped white tail and a wing-long blaze of white in the dark wings. With almost the communal precision of sandpipers, the flock may wheel and bank in unison; a kaleidoscope of black and white.

36 Family *Charadriidae*
PLOVERS, TURNSTONES, and the SURFBIRD

Plovers are compact, plump-bodied shorebirds or waders with large heads and large eyes — the large eyes are surprising in a group that is active primarily in daytime. The bills of plovers, lapwings, and the surfbird bear superficial resemblance to that of a pigeon's. That is, the base is leathery and expands slightly into a horny tip.

The aberrant species known as turnstones have the bill modified into a diminutive upturned version of an oystercatcher's except more acute at the tip. It is used, as the bird's name indicates, to flip over pebbles along the shore in search of the invertebrates that might be hidden underneath.

Members of the plover family have been touted as classic examples of "concealing coloration,"and "distraction display," and "injury-feigning." Certainly those who know the small piping plover will agree that its dry-sand-colored back, white belly lost in shadow, and the strategically placed disruptive pattern of black virtually obliterate it on the beach. Watch its swift run over the dry sand until it comes to an abrupt, motionless halt — let your eyes stray from it ever so slightly and until it moves you will be lucky if you can pick it up again.

The same is true of the darker, more boldly marked ring plover. *Its* back is of the color of *wet* sand in harmony with its preference for mud flats and wet, sandy beaches.

Many and possibly all of the plovers perform the most convincing histrionics. They pretend to be crippled and hobble away with flailing wings in an effort to distract predatory animals away from their eggs or young. Many a

111

Black-bellied Plover   ad ♂
(Squatarola squatarola)
Khantaak I. Yakutat, Alaska.
May 16, 1936

small boy, ambling through a pasture, has been startled by the sudden appearance of a fluttering, crawling, "wounded" killdeer. Attempting in sympathy to catch it, he is dumbfounded when, after being led a merry chase for forty or fifty yards, the bird with the broken wing and leg lifts effortlessly into the air, flies to a safe distance, and alights in a twinkling run on perfectly sound limbs.

Ringed plover feigning injury (distraction display)

The larger members of the plover family — lapwings — are more strikingly colored and many possess rakish, curling crests, wattles about the mouth and eyes, and large, sharp spurs at the bend of the wings. The best known of this group in the New World is the téru-téru, a handsome grey-brown-backed bird with black forehead, throat, and chest, with a thin crest of a few black feathers curving upward from the nape. Its range is from Colombia to Argentina. It is frequently seen near human habitation, and its loud cry is as familiar in the pastures there as the killdeer's in North America.

◄ *Black-bellied plover*

113

37 Family *Thinocoridae*
SEEDSNIPE

Little is known about this strictly South American family, made up of only four species. Anatomically they represent an admixture of attributes, each usually associated with other unrelated and widely divergent families.

Start with a beak that closely resembles a bunting's, but add a scaly, opercular flap over the nostrils like that found in the quails; continue with the crop of a chicken and short legs like a turnstone's but with the tarsus reticulate (that is, covered by small hexagonal scales closely packed together like the cells in a honey bee's comb), a condition found in the thick-knees and some plovers; finish off by adding the wings and tail of a snipe.

Bring our fanciful bird to life and it runs over the ground like a short-legged plover, bobs its head back and forth like a dove, and feeds on the seeds of grasses and dwarf plants like a ground finch.

If alarmed it drops to the ground and flattens out with head and neck fully extended and pressed closely against the earth in a concealment venture similar to that of the thick-knees; then, when it senses that it has been detected, it leaps into the air and flies off with the erratic, winding, turning flight of a snipe.

Though recognizing all these look-alikes, my impression of seedsnipe is that, in the field, they most resemble a cross between one of the smaller sandgrouse and the Fischer's sparrow-lark of Africa — no wonder their exact placement in the avian scheme of things is, to say the least, controversial.

All seedsnipe live in dry tundra-like regions from the seacoasts of the Falkland Islands and Patagonia through the dry, barren portions of the pampas to the wind-swept high altitudes of the Paramo of Peru and Ecuador. It is thought that the opercular flap covering the nostrils may be a shield against the cutting, blowing sand and dust of their blustery habitat.

Gay's seedsnipe of the Paramo is large — about dove-sized — and beautifully patterned in concentric rings of brown on each breast feather.

Gay's seedsnipe in ichu grass

38 Family *Scolopacidae*
SNIPES, SANDPIPERS, etc.

This is a family of close to one hundred world species. Included in it are many more or less distinctive branches with their own accepted group names: woodcocks, snipes, tattlers, curlews, godwits, stints, and so on. The most significant difference between these birds and the plovers is in the slenderness and the peculiar *sensitiveness* of the beak. The beak is soft-skinned throughout, and, in feeding, the birds probe and even *feel* with it. Much of the food of many species lives in murky water or wet mud and is located by the tactile percipience of the bill. It can be short and straight as in the stints; long and straight as in the tattlers; very long and straight with a flexible, somewhat prehensile tip as in the snipes and woodcocks; long and strongly downcurved as in the curlews; long and mildly upturned as in the godwits.

The relationship between these birds is readily recognized through familiarity with the birds in life, but it is not easily put into words. All have long, slender legs and are inhabitants of the edges of wet spots and marshes, the shores of pools, ponds, tarns, creeks, brooks, rivers, lakes, seas, and oceans.

Nature, of course, provides exceptions to any rule that we may contrive and some "sandpipers" are almost strictly upland birds — for example, the upland plover (which is *not* a plover and should be called the Bartramian sandpiper, or, better still, the upland sandpiper — or maybe even the colloquial "quaillie" from its quivering calls). It was formerly common in the virgin grasslands; with their disappearance it adjusted to

Woodcock ▶

116

Woodcock ♂
Philohela minor
Pelee Island, Lake Erie
October, 1951.

rich pasture lands and hay meadows; now one looks for it on the grass strips between runways at airports.

We have said that the members of this family have long legs. We can add that they also have long necks, that the wings are long and pointed, and that the head and eyes are small. All this might be fine were it not for the existence of the woodcock. Its neck and legs are not long; its wings are short and rounded; its head is large and its eyes are enormous. Not only that, but the eyes protrude and are far back and high up on the head, directly above its ears. They are located in such a strange position that the posterior binocular field is much wider than the anterior. Don't scoff at the old witticism about "eyes in the back of the head" — nature has given it a try and found it useful!

Most members of the *Scolopacidae* are highly gregarious in the non-breeding seasons. Many undertake prodigious mass migrations from the high arctic to winter in extreme southern South America. They very nearly live in perpetual daylight. Some species perform song flights on their nesting grounds in the far north, and the musical quality of their voices comes as a surprise to those familiar only with the conversational gabble or the alarm cries of migrating flocks.

Rock sandpiper

118

39 Family *Recurvirostridae*
AVOCETS and STILTS

The first time I saw a long-legged, delicate-looking avocet glide down and prepare to make a landing in deep water, I held my breath, thinking the bird had made a misjudgment. I was surprised to see it land lightly and swim off with all the aplomb of a duck. I learned later that the avocet is remarkably well equipped to be a swimmer as well as a wading bird.

The body is slightly flattened like a duck's and covered with a dense duck-like plumage. The toes are fully webbed. The American avocet prefers alkaline pools and lakes where it feeds on small aquatic animal life using a sweeping motion of the long acute bill. The bill is curved, sometimes strongly, upward and ends in a hooked tip. A beautifully pied black-and-white bird, a soft shade of cinnamon or chestnut invades the neck and head. If its appearance is impressive, so also is its clamor when its home territory is invaded. A second species is confined to the salt lakes of the Andes.

The beak of the stilt is more ordinary — long and straight, very slightly upcurved, tapering to a sharp point. It is more of a prober. Its legs are the longest in relation to body size of any bird, as remarkable for their slenderness as for their length. The legs are a stunningly beautiful shade of geranium pink. The whole bird presents an appearance of slender, willowy delicacy. Duck hunters might dispute this. In the Middle West they are known in the colloquial as lawyers — because like avocets, they talk a lot and, sharp-eyed, often sound a vociferous alarm that has ruined many a stealthy stalk of wild ducks.

119

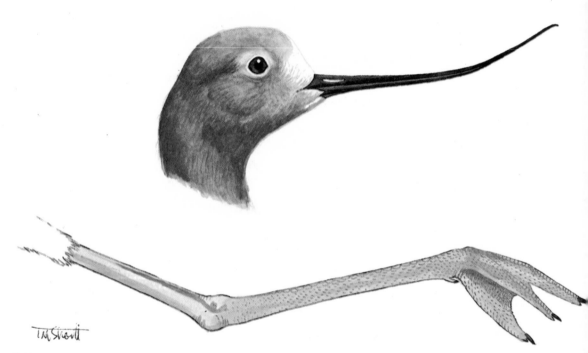

TM Shortt

Pelican Lake Manitoba - May 28, 1944   Recurvirostra americana , American Avocet ♂

Black-necked stilt

To me, stilts are somehow suggestive of a small boy on stilts (obviously others thought so too and so named them). In addition to the stilt-like legs, there is a resemblance when walking, of the way the lifted leg inclines backwards to the nearly horizontal and bends back on itself at the "ankle," to the way a boy's elbows bend as he holds the tops of his stilts.

◄ *American avocet*

40 PHALAROPES
Family *Phalaropodidae*

The name "phalarope" was coined from the Greek words *phalarus*, a coot, and *pous*, a foot: coot-footed, with reference to the lobate toes similar to those of the coots. The three phalarope species are small, sandpiper-like birds of even more delicate appearance than sandpipers. Owing to the thick, compact plumage of the breast and belly which gives their bodies a falsely plump look, the small head and slender beak seem almost out of proportion.

Phalaropes are classic examples of sex role reversal. The females are larger and more brightly colored than the males and perform most of the courtship rituals. The males incubate the eggs and care for the young which, covered with copious fluffy down, leave the nest hours after hatching. I suspect that the females take a more active interest in the nest and young than is generally conceded. On two occasions, once with red-necked and once with red phalaropes, I found a female at the nest at dusk. It may be that the females, being more conspicuous, take at least part of the night shift.

Phalaropes are notably fearless when brooding (and indeed often at other times.) Once at a nest of a red-necked phalarope I found the male sitting. Desirous of seeing the eggs, I gently slid two fingers under his chest and raised him so that I could see the four eggs. His only reaction was to raise his back and scapular feathers in a "with his hackles up" gesture and to peck gently at my fingers.

The feathers of the breast and belly of phalaropes are so numerous and grow so closely together that instead of lying

flat and overlapping each other as in most birds, they stand out
almost vertically from the body and curl at the ends for their
overlap. This provides such a deep layer of feathery insulation
that it makes phalaropes among the lightest of birds for their
apparent body bulk. As a result, when swimming they float
like corks on top of the water rather than partly in it. It also
accounts for the ease with which they spin and whirligig as,
with stiffly held necks, they pick their food from the surface. A
large part of their food is mosquito and other aquatic insect
larvae.

When summer ends the red-necked and red phalaropes
undergo a dramatic transformation in their life-style, perhaps
more so than any other bird: large flocks go out to sea, far out
of sight of land, swimming buoyantly on the billowing swells
and feeding on marine plankton — their only avian
companions the storm petrels, shearwaters, and albatrosses,
and sometimes a jaeger or skua.

Wilson's phalarope is more of a landlubber and winters in
the interior as far south as Argentina.

Wilson's phalarope

Double-striped Thick-knee
Burhinus bistriatus

41 Family *Burhinidae*
THICK-KNEES or STONE CURLEWS

These large birds suggest oversized, robust plovers — or small slender bustards — which is not surprising for they are related to both. The interchangeable English names — thick-knees and stone curlews — are both unfortunate. The almost universal misapprehension that a bird's instep is its leg and that the first joint we see is its knee bending backward instead of forward has been responsible for much confusion and faulty nomenclature.

They are running birds with long, strong legs and, like many cursorial groups, have only three short stout toes. When excited they have a habit of "bobbing" — ducking the head and jerking the tail up. To conform with their mostly nocturnal habits they have proportionately large eyes. The eyes are of various tints of golden yellow and, by virtue of the peculiarities of the eyelids and surrounding feathers, have an alert and piercing look.

In flight they resemble large plovers, being long and powerful of wing. They often fly at considerable heights. During the day thick-knees rest on the ground with their legs tucked under their bodies. They then resemble a large stone. Since they often choose rocky places to rest, they are almost invisible unless by sheer chance one happens to see a big golden eye. They seem to be well aware of their protective camouflage and often, rather than fly, will drop flat among the stones and squat with head and neck fully extended and pressed down against the ground. When thus concealed they

◄ *Double-striped thick-knee*

will allow close approach, putting full reliance on their ability to merge with their surroundings.

Three species occur in warm temperate and tropical America, one of which, the double-striped thick-knee, occurs north to southern Mexico and inhabits the arid savannas and semi-deserts of the isthmus of Tehuantepec. Its food consists of small animals that emerge at dusk — slugs, large insects, worms, and occasionally even a mouse, a small lizard, or a nestling bird.

Double-striped thick-knee

Young thick-knees are among the most precocious of all birds; hatching fully "clothed" from very large eggs, they are running about within minutes of hatching.

Double-striped thick-knees frequently gather in small flocks at dusk and fly about after dark, uttering unworldly cackling sounds as they course back and forth over pasture lands or other open areas.

42 Family *Stercorariidae*
JAEGERS and SKUA

Their webbed toes with sharp, curved talons and their long beaks with tearing, hawk-like hooked tips, admirably equip these gull-like birds to play the role of sea hawk. There are four species: three are called jaegers (from the German *jäger*, a hunter) and are of circumpolar distribution; the fourth is a large, dark brown, gull-like bird called a skua (from its old Norse name *skúfr*). The skua has the most divided range among birds, being the only species to breed in both the arctic and the antarctic. The separate populations move to warmer oceanic waters in their respective winters. The arctic birds, which nest only on the European side of the Atlantic, move into the North Atlantic; the more widely ranging antarctic nesters drift into all oceans at the opposite time of year. So it is that, although of one species and barely distinguishable, the birds of the two divisions probably never meet each other.

In the New World skuas nest along the cold, barren coasts of southern Chile, but to see them one must follow the fishing fleets off the coasts of Chile, Peru, and Ecuador in the Humboldt Current. Here, the fishing nets are attended by hordes of guanays, boobies, and brown pelicans; by frigatebirds, gulls, and terns. Amidst the frenzied activity of these milling throngs attracted by the masses of fish brought up by the nets, one may see the large, dark skuas flying about the periphery with their calm yet powerful wing-beats. Occasionally they pick up a fish but usually, being pirates, they force a booby or a gull to drop or disgorge its prize, hard-earned in the avian rummage-sale.

(*Stercorarius parasiticus*)
Parasitic Jaeger ♀
  Black Glacier, Malaspina,
    July 6, 1936.
      (1 year old ?)

Skua

Jaegers are more familiar to North American bird-watchers but even so a sighting is a red letter day unless the observer travels to their arctic breeding grounds. Most jaegers spend the winter wandering at sea. A few straggle south into the interior as far as the Great Lakes.

The three species come in large, medium, and small sizes and are best distinguished by the length and shape of the two central tail feathers.

All members of the family are truly birds of prey, capable of capturing living creatures, although their robbing and scavenging habits earn them their infamous reputation as buccaneers. I once saw a parasitic jaeger pursue a juvenile least sandpiper in flight; it followed every evasive twist and turn as the little bird tried desperately to escape. The jaeger soon overtook it and snapped it out of the air with its beak, then lapsed into its normal, slow flight throwing back its head and swallowing its victim whole.

◀ *Parasitic jaeger*

43 SKIMMERS

Family *Rynchopidae*

The architecture of the bills of many kinds of birds arouses our wonder, but surely the most unconventional of all is that of the skimmer. Here, the lower mandible is longer than the upper and is compressed like the blade of a dinner knife. Its end is obtuse. Its sides come abruptly together and for much of their length are fused. Its top edge is sharp, inset into a groove in the upper mandible. The dissected-out lower jawbone, looked at separately, resembles a short-handled, two-pronged pitchfork.

The upper mandible is also compressed and is nearly hollow, with an internal porous structure. It is singular in that it is fastened to the forehead by a ductile hinge that enables it to move freely up and down — all this is an adaptation to the birds' peculiar manner of obtaining their food.

The wings are uncommonly long and the flight more measured and sweeping than that of the terns to which they are closely related. They fly in close formation, moving simultaneously rather than in straggly companies like terns. They seem to feed as they skim low over the water with their foreparts inclined slightly downward and with the blade-like lower mandible grazing or cutting the water's surface. The exact mechanics of how they capture prey while so engaged is still controversial, but it appears that when the lower mandible comes in contact with a fish the upper blade of the bill is triggered to close; the fish is flipped out and swallowed as the bird proceeds on its swift way without even pausing.

Black skimmer

This is not the end of "believe it or nots" about these surprising birds. They also bark like dogs and have "cat's eyes"! The voice resembles the sharp *arf* of a puppy and the pupils of the eyes are vertically elliptical when contracted, rather than round as in all other birds.

In the New World, skimmers breed in colonies, often numbering in the thousands — on beaches, saltings, and estuaries — from New Jersey in the East and coastal Mexico in the West to Argentina and Chile.

Black skimmer ▶

TmShortt—

Black Skimmer ♂
Rynchops niger
Pointe-a-Pierre, Trinida
May 1957

Forktailed Gull ♂
Galápagos, Santa Cruz
April 1965

44 Family *Laridae*
GULLS and TERNS

This group of long-winged web-footed water birds is so familiar to almost everyone that little elaboration of their external characteristics is necessary. About a hundred species, slightly more than half of them terns, inhabit almost every coastline and freshwater lake in the world. *Laridae* divide into two generally well-marked subfamilies — the gulls and the terns.

Terns are smaller, though the largest species are bigger than the smallest gulls. Terns' beaks are long and acutely pointed for spear-diving their prey, rather than coarse and hooked as the gulls' beaks. Their legs are very short and they walk poorly, whereas gulls' legs are adequate for walking. The wings of terns are proportionately even longer and much more pointed. But their habits and behavior distinguish them more expressly than their anatomy.

Terns are essentially hunters of living prey, which they obtain by diving on it from the wing. Gulls are basically scavengers. They spend most of their time eating or cruising the shores looking for something to eat. Anything alive, dying, or dead is a potential food source.

The *Laridae* are cosmopolitan and, in general, large numbers are found together: at nesting grounds, on migration, or in winter when their association depends upon community interest in the matter of food.

One of the most singular of gulls is the elegant fork-tailed gull of the Galápagos Islands. It is possibly the only habitually nocturnal gull in the world, feeding largely on squid which

◄   *Fork-tailed gull*

come to the surface at night. Living as it does on the sheer lava cliff faces of the islands, it has developed a form of "echo-location" similar to that of bats. The response from the emission of a series of rapid clicking sounds as it approaches its perpendicular home enables it to gauge its nearness.

Aleutian tern

Many species of gulls have a red, red and black, or black spot on the side of their yellow bills. This serves as a trigger — when a gull chick pecks at the conspicuous blaze it prompts the adult to regurgitate food. In the fork-tailed gull the trigger is a round white spot amid the black feathers near the base of the bill — red or black would be invisible in the dark and of no value to the hungry chick.

Both gulls and terns are fierce defenders of their eggs, young, and territory. It is a stoical person indeed who can refrain from ducking as they power-dive at his head amid a tumult of harsh, angry gull voices.

45 Family *Alcidae*
AUKS, MURRES, and PUFFINS

Alcidae are three-toed (the hind toe wanting), web-footed seabirds of the rocky coasts of the northern hemisphere. All are large-headed, short-tailed, short-legged, and small-winged. There are twenty-two species, most confined to the north Pacific coasts and islands. Their black-and-white plumage, upright stance, and use of wings in swimming under water has caused considerable confusion with the southern hemisphere penguins; but these resemblances are entirely superficial; they are actually much more closely related to gulls. Their outward similarity to penguins is a striking example of convergent evolution, and shows why adaptive characters must be used with much caution in classification systems.

Although all members of the family agree closely in essential respects, they differ among themselves to an unparalleled degree in the form of the bill. This frequently assumes an odd shape, has horny processes, is decorated with ridges or furrows, or is brilliantly colored. A number of species are remarkable for the extraordinary changes that the bill undergoes. Parts of the horny covering or sheath are regularly shed or moulted in a manner analagous to the shedding of a deer's antlers. In the tufted puffin, for example, no fewer than seven brightly colored horny pieces fall off separately after the breeding season is over, leaving a dull, dark, winter beak, little more than half the size of the spring and summer beak. The small horny processes about the eye are also shed and the brightly colored, fleshy rosette at the corner of the mouth

◀ *Tufted puffin*

Kittlitz's murrelet

shrinks and discolors. A further transformation ensues with the shedding of the long, downy, corn-colored crests and the replacement of the white facial feathers by dusky ones. In the tufted puffin the change from breeding to winter dress is one of the most dramatic among birds.

All species of *Alcidae* walk badly and some scarcely at all. The position of the legs in relation to the axis of the body is such that they must assume an upright posture in standing, which they do by resting on their rumps with the feet extended out in front, the whole of the tarsus and toes touching the ground. (Puffins and one or two others stand well on their toes and walk with less difficulty.)

In spite of their small wings, all existing species fly well with a rapid, vigorous motion of the wings, propelled by large and powerful pectoral muscles. The largest of all alcids, the now extinct great auk, was flightless, a circumstance that contributed largely to its extermination.

138

46
Family *Columbidae*
PIGEONS and DOVES

The many geographical units bearing the name "Columbia" may well have been so named for a pigeon, for *columba* is Latin for a dove or pigeon. Was Christopher Columbus's family name derived from that source? Whether or not, many idioms in the English language have their origins in fancied attributes of pigeons, most of them erroneous: "pigeon-hearted" (faint-hearted) — pigeons are really quite courageous as non-predatory birds go; "pigeon pair" (boy and girl twins or boy and girl as only children) — on the mistaken assumption that pigeons raised one male and one female at a nesting; "pigeon-livered" (quiet, affable) — pigeons are noisy and irascible; "dove of peace" — few birds are less qualified: they are aggressively amorous and, while tender and devoted to their young, their love is marked by irritability and pugnacity. Much of the chaste image ascribed to pigeons owes its origin to the writings of early authors who, noting the absence of a gall bladder in these birds, assumed they were without bile or rancour! Perhaps the only simile that is valid is "pigeon-toed."

The names "pigeon" and "dove" are interchangeable and do not imply any difference other than the usual application of "dove" to the smaller members of the family. Remember that the wild ancestor of the domestic *pigeon* is the rock *dove*.

Some three hundred kinds of pigeons are known to exist. They are most abundant in the New Guinea region where more than one fourth of the species occur. Wallace accounted for this in the absence of fruit-eating monkeys and squirrels — competitors for food and also predators of eggs and young.

♀

♂

~ T M Shortt

Galápagos Doves.
<u>Nesopelia galapagoensis</u>
Isla Santiago, Galápagos
May. 1965.

Bills of some individuals
much decurved. Those depicted
above most commonly recurring
bell shape.

Inca dove

Conversely, pigeons are relatively few in species and numbers in the forests of South America and are represented to a large extent by ground-inhabiting species which nest in low bushes where monkeys and tree rodents do not habitually descend. Fewer than a dozen kinds have penetrated and remained as North American birds, yet what was once possibly the most abundant bird in the world — the North American passenger pigeon — is now extinct. Much has been written about its vast migrating flocks which blotted out the sun, but perhaps the most poignant documents are contracts for hired hands containing a clause stipulating that the help should not be fed "too often on wild pigeons or salmon."

A unique feature of pigeons is that the gullet is distended to form a capacious crop, the skin of which secretes a special milky fluid — pigeon's milk — which, mixed with chewed, regurgitated food, is poured directly into the mouths of the young.

◄ *Galápagos dove*

47 Family *Cuculidae* CUCKOOS

The first known written verse of the English language, composed about A.D. 1250 (according to Bartlett's *Anthology*), was a brief outburst in admiration of a cuckoo:

> *Sumer is icumen in,*
> *Lhude sing cuccu!*
> *Groweth sed and bloweth med,*
> *And Springeth the wud nu —*
> *Sing cuccu!*

Fanciful and not so fanciful attributes have been given the cuckoo — from its role as the harbinger of summer, down to the cuckold, the deceived husband of an unfaithful wife, and the more modern "cuckoo," meaning daft. As well as being famous for laying its eggs in other birds' nests, the species responsible for all of the above and much more is the common cuckoo of Europe which is but one of more than 120 species of cuckoos found in nearly all the warmer parts of the world. It should be noted that only about forty-five or fifty kinds are brood-parasites — like the common cuckoo — and that most of these are Old World forms.

The best known American cuckoos, the black-billed cuckoo and the yellow-billed cuckoo, though not habitually parasitic, do occasionally slip an egg into another bird's nest or, more frequently, into each other's. One species of American cuckoo, the smooth-billed ani, experiments with a communistic nesting colony in which several birds unite in building a large nest to be used by all. Two dozen or more eggs may be deposited by several females. Those laid first (and therefore on the bottom of the pile) often are not sufficiently incubated and fail to hatch. Having shared nest-building and incubation chores, the several females all care for the young.

The most outstanding of American cuckoos are the two large terrestrial roadrunners of the arid regions from

Squirrel cuckoo

southwestern U.S.A. to Peru. Though less than two feet long (half of which is tail), few birds run as swiftly as these ground cuckoos. Aided by the half-opened wings acting as outriggers, they can sprint at better than fifteen miles an hour.

They feed on snakes, lizards, small mammals, and such large invertebrates as land molluscs, grasshoppers, and beetles; in fact, all the pests which early settlers did not want around their homes. Therefore, instead of cats, the homesteaders often tamed a young roadrunner and kept it both as a pet and as a vermin exterminator.

48 Family *Psittacidae*
PARROTS

With both beak and feet highly prehensile, parrots climb better than any other kind of bird. They are to birds what monkeys are to mammals; the parallel can be drawn further by their fruit-eating habit and by their cantankerous and mischievous temperament.

The short, strong legs and yoked toes (that is, two toes directed forward and two turned backward) provide a vise-like grip for climbing and a tool for picking up food and conveying it to the mouth. The tongue is thick and fleshy and has a horny outgrowth on the underside like a human fingernail. Objects can be handled skillfully between the tongue and the sharply hooked upper mandible which is hinged rather than sutured to the skull, and so is freely movable. The lower mandible is short and thick — a "thumb" opposed to the "finger" of the upper. So, in addition to gripping food items in the manner of a lobster's claw, the bill can be used in climbing like a human hand.

The voices of parrots are the most hideous of all bird sounds — grating, strident, and squawky — always discordant. Yet the ability to articulate human speech is one of their notorious talents (but perhaps this is not a contradiction). Exclusively peculiar structural formations of the syrinx and the muscles controlling the tongue are responsible. It should be added that they are simply mimicking sounds that they hear in the same way that starlings ape the voices of other birds.

Thick-billed parrot ▶

144

TMShortt

Thickbilled Parrot ♀
    Rhynchopsitta pachyrhyncha.
  nr Cumbre, Chihuahua, Mexico
        Aug 1946.

49 Family *Tytonidae*
BARN OWL

The common barn owl is more frequently associated with human habitation than other owls. It is a persistent inhabitant of old buildings, gables, and church towers. It may be said that it haunts them, for, crepuscular and nocturnal, it is a will-o-the-wisp, appearing as a noiseless shadow and vanishing furtively — its pinions make no sound in flight.

The underparts of its body and wings are white and add to its ghostly appearance as it reels and wavers through the dusk. It was undoubtedly the archetype of the floating, sheet-clad image of a wraith. To appreciate this one must see a barn owl at dark about one of its favorite haunts, an old church tower with a belfry, in which it has its nest. Picture the superstitious person passing the neglected and moldering graveyard that is usually associated with old churches, who gets a glimpse of a silent, white apparition that wafts over the headstones and vanishes behind a crumbling wall; and a moment later there comes a snoring sound followed by moaning shrieks and screams! We can be sure that our credulous hero is now outstripping the wind.

In all likelihood it is also responsible for the opprobrium that for centuries has been associated, in the western world, with all owls — that they are birds of ill omen. This belief was already firmly established in Europe in Shakespeare's time and he makes use of it in *Hamlet*, *Titus Andronicus*, and especially in *Macbeth* where Harpier, the owl, plays a strong supporting role in the murder scene. Strangely enough, owls are looked upon as birds of wisdom and favorable augury by the peoples of primitive societies.

The distinctive, heart-shaped facial discs surrounding the small very dark eyes have given the barn owl the vernacular "monkey-face." These feather tracts are more complete and distinct than those of other owls and act as sound-focalizing parabolas for the enormous ears which lie beneath them. Experimental work has shown that barn owls are capable of detecting the presence of mice and capturing them through hearing alone, unaided by sight.

Barn owl

The common barn owl is very nearly cosmopolitan, being absent only from the colder parts of the northern and southern hemispheres. In less civilized parts of the world, it makes its home in dark woods, on rocky hillsides, and in mountainous regions. In wilder country where there are no man-made edifices such as windmills, barns, granaries, dilapidated buildings, and ruins, it nests in cavities of almost any type.

Barn owl ▶

TMShortt

Barn Owl ♀? *Tyto alba hellm*
near Curepe, Trinidad.
May 1957.

Live, uninjured bird, later released.
Sex by size only.

Spectacled Owl ♂
Pulsatrix perspicillata
Mt. El Tucuché
Trinidad
May 1957

Head feathers highly erectile.
Sometimes looks almost like
a Crested Eagle, at others
feathers are so flattened
as to give a "no forehead"
look.

Bill appears to be
very large, proportionately.
Possibly partly because of sparsity
of nasal plumes compared with
more boreal species.

Dense Tropical Rain Forest.

50 Family *Strigidae*
TYPICAL OWLS

In recent years owls have enjoyed an immense popularity (of which the birds themselves are totally unaware). There are numerous collectors of owls, whose objets d'art range from soapstone ookpiks and owls cast in bronze, to owls made of wool and pipe-cleaners, of nuts and seashells. They amass paintings, prints, sculptures, carvings, and batiks of owls; owls made of cloth, or glass, of ceramic, leather, plastic or fibre; felt cutouts and decals of owls. Some things appeal to the human whimsy to a much greater degree than others; some are basically amusing either in appearance or inference, as comedians have been quick to learn. An onion, for example is funny; a head of lettuce isn't. Owls' eyes — large, looking forward, set in circlets of radiating feathers known as facial discs — impart a semblance of reflective wisdom that is perhaps a caricature of a human face.

Whatever the reason, the current vogue is not new: it is a rebirth of the fascination primitive peoples and early civilizations had and have for the birds of darkness. The screech owl and the horned owl were prominent in the art and ritual of the Mayans of Yucatan. They appear in the pottery pipes of the Mound Builders of the Hopewell culture of Ohio. An owl was the sign M in the Egyptian hieroglyphic. The little owl was the constant companion of Athene, the owl-eyed maiden goddess of the Greeks. The myth of the wisdom of the human-faced owl is deep-rooted and still persists.

The external ears of owls are extremely large and in most species are provided with a movable flap or operculum. The

◀ *Spectacled owl*

150

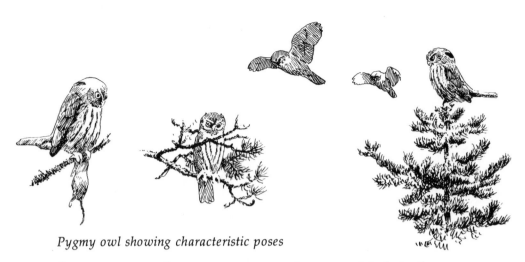

Pygmy owl showing characteristic poses

flap represents the nearest approach among birds to the ear-conch of mammals. The plumicorns or feathery "horns" commonly referred to as "ears" (long-eared owl and short-eared owl, for example) are strictly tufts of lengthened feathers rising from the forehead above the eyes and have nothing whatsoever to do with hearing, although their fancied resemblance to the devil's horns had much to do with their former undeserved reputation as evil spirits.

In some species of owls (barred owl and spotted owl) the ears are different on the two sides of the head, with the right ear distinctly larger and of a different shape than the left. The ears of the long-eared and short-eared owls have enormous openings that occupy the whole sides of the head; a fold of skin divides the outer ear into two chambers: one contains the true ear opening or tympanum, the other encloses a blind chamber. On the right side of the head the true ear opening is in the lower chamber, while on the left side the positions are exactly reversed with the true ear opening in the upper chamber!

Overshadowing even this complexity is the difference in shape of the ears of the little boreal owl and the saw-whet owl, wherein it is so great that the skull itself is lopsided and asymmetrical, an extremely rare circumstance in animals.

Great grey owl ▶

Great Grey Owl ♀
Strix nebulosa
Flat Creek, Yukon
Oct 2, 1944 .

Shorteared Owl. ♀
Asio flammeus galápagoensis
Isla Santa Cruz, Galápagos
2400 ft.

Dark Galápagos race. Back almost uniformly dark
brown.; tarsal feathers marked with streaks.
belly feathers striped and barred.

Like continental race, wings raised high in upstroke, shallow on downward

51 OILBIRD

Family *Steatornithidae*

This family was set up to accommodate its sole member, the bizarre oilbird or guacharo (Venezuelan Indian for "wailer") of Trinidad, Venezuela, Guyana, through Colombia to Ecuador and Peru. The oilbird is strictly nocturnal; related on the one hand to the owls and on the other to the nightjars. It differs from both and from most other birds in the possession of well-developed olfactory organs suggesting that it has an efficient sense of smell.

Oilbirds live in subterranean grottos and chambers in long, deep caves where no light ever penetrates. Their only companions are bats, camel crickets, eyeless fish, blind salamanders, sightless crustaceans, beetles, and flatworms. Oilbirds spend the daytime hours in total darkness, rear their young, and fly about without inconvenience — this because of their highly developed sonar echo-location capabilities. They send out a stream of short, high-pitched pulses, low enough for detection by the human ear, but still about four and a half octaves above middle C. This can be heard as a continuous clicking sound. Combined with the other snarling, groaning, chaffering sounds that they utter, an oilbird colony in the inky blackness is an eerie place.

Oilbirds emerge after darkness envelops the forests surrounding their cave. They can now make use of the large night-seeing eyes that seemed anomalous in the cave. With a two-and-a-half-foot wingspread, they may fly for miles to stands of certain palm trees where, with their strong, hooked

◀ *Galápagos short-eared owl*

bills, they detach the palm nuts while hovering in the air. The nuts are swallowed whole and digested during the day when the birds are back in their dark dungeons.

Guacharo

Young oilbirds grow enormously fat on the same nuts which are carried to them by their parents. Until recently this condition seriously endangered the existence of the species since the young were taken by the native peoples, just before they could fly, for their fat which was rendered out and used as a cooking oil. Most of the known caves are now under some form of protection.

TMShortt

Oilbird or Guacharo ♀
Steatornis caripensis
Mt. Aripo, Trinidad
May 1957.

TMShortt

Grey Potoo ♀. "Poor-me-one"
Nyctibius griseus.
El Tucuché, Trinidad
May 1957

52 POTOOS

Family *Nyctibiidae*

In Trinidad and northern South America, one of the pleasant sounds issuing from the edge of the rain forest is the call of the "poor-me-one," (patois for the grey potoo and which can be interpreted as "poor me, alone"). The words approximate about as closely to the song as such things are possible — one can't spell out in letters a phrase on a flute or a violin. It is one of the unforgettable ariettas of the velvety black night of the tropics, sung to the accompaniment of the strings of the night stridulators, the crickets and grasshoppers, and the woodwinds of the tree frogs.

In daytime one *looks at* grey potoos much more often than one *sees* them. Their resting position is almost vertically upright and usually on an old branch scar where a limb, before dropping off, has bent the main branch slightly away from it. The potoo, in effect, becomes the "broken stub" where the limb had been. Its marvellously concealing color and pattern, of wood greys and browns, blend it imperceptibly into the bark. The long tail is pressed closely against the identically colored trunk, the eyes are half-closed, and the head points upward with its feathers tightly compressed. Its oneness with its perch must be seen to be believed, but discovering it is not an easy feat. Dr. George Miksch Sutton, the famous naturalist, writes: "While climbing a slope above the Rio Sabinas in southern Tamaulipas I grasped at a slender stump for support only to have the whole top of it fly off — a potoo, no less!"

◀ Top: *Guacharo*
Bottom: *Grey potoo*

53 NIGHTJARS

Family *Caprimulgidae*

Many a person (including me) lying in his tent in the darkness after a long day on the trail or in the canoe has been delighted to hear that he has pitched his camp within the territory of a whip-poor-will. He lies there marvelling at the clear enunciation and thinking that this is one bird whose voice lends itself ideally to onomatopoeia. An hour or so later, as the whip-poor-will begins its sixth or seventh series of no-pause, hundred-plus reiterations of its name, the enchantment palls and ears are covered in an attempt to escape the "whip-poor-wills." Few birds are so repetitious.

The family to which it belongs is alternately known as the nightjars (derived from the "churring" sounds of several species — "jarring" the night air) or goatsuckers, a nonsense name that should be discontinued as it has its origin in the preposterous myth that the birds sucked the milk of nanny goats until they were dry. Normally dry nannies coming in after a hot summer evening, during which a few nightjars might have been seen flying about amidst the goat flock and hawking the flies attracted by the notoriously malodorous animals, prompted the accusation. Since a nightjar stomach might hold a teaspoonful, it would require a queue of about eighty "goatsuckers" drinking in rapid succession to drain a good milch nanny (never mind that their mouths possess no sucking lips).

The nightjars form an almost cosmopolitan family, absent only from the very cold regions. They are medium-sized birds, all characterized by small and weak bills and feet. They are strong of wing and provided with an enormous mouth which opens up to below the eye and in some species beyond it. The mouth is edged by long stiff bristles — an efficient fly-trap.

The plumage is soft, loose, and fluffy as in owls and they are cryptically colored in shades and tones matching their resting places: woodland species are of browns, buffs, and tans; rain forest types are generally darker; desert dwellers are the color of sand.

Rufous-collared nightjar

Most kinds fly low over pasture edges and open areas in woodlots or forests, capturing flying insects on the wing.

The American nighthawks are different. They have no bristles about the gape and they fly high, often over towns and cities, having thoroughly adjusted themselves to metropolitan life. The general aspect of flat gravel-covered roofs studded with chimneys, TV aerials, and other vertical prominences is the same as an old burn or a jack pine barren on granitic rock — the American nighthawk's natural environment.

54 Family *Apodidae*
SWIFTS

Swifts are wide-headed, muscular little birds with long, bowed wings and are remarkable for their powers of flight. The speed of their straightaway flight is unequalled even by the fastest of falcons. Contributing to this prowess is a characteristic that they share with hummingbirds and has to do with the relative length of the wing-bones. The "arm" and "forearm" are extremely short and thick; the "hand" notably elongated. This means that the feather part of the wing is made up mainly of long, stiff primary flight-feathers which spring from the "hand."

It is a commonplace sight, even over cities, to see scores or hundreds of swifts sweeping the sky in pursuit of flying insects, usually at dawn or dusk and often before or after a thunderstorm. When they have finished feeding and are ready to return to their nests or roosts, swifts engage in a kind of aerial play. A huge flock races back and forth uttering at intervals a literal bedlam of twittering noise. They wheel and sail in unison, then suddenly take off again, their wingbeats so rapid as to appear blurred.

Many American species, including the chimney swift, belong to the group know as spine-tailed swifts. Their short tail-feathers have the shafts extended as sharp, bare spines like the tips of common pins. The appearance of these swifts in flight, usually high in the air, has given them the vernacular of "flying cigars." Swifts are cavity nesters that attach their nests to vertical surfaces such as the walls of a hollow tree or the interior of a man-made chimney.

Cayenne swift

A remarkable point in the structure of swifts is in the great development of their salivary glands. The secretion thus produced is used as a glue by which small twigs are joined together and stuck to the wall in nest building. In one Oriental species the whole nest is made of congealed saliva—and is the source of the famous edible bird's nest and its derivative, bird's nest soup.

The nidification of some tropical species is unusual. The cayenne swift builds a tubular sleeve, often two feet in length and open at the lower end. It is made entirely of downy seeds (like milkweed) and other plant down gathered by the birds while on the wing and cemented together with saliva. It is built on the underside of a large tree limb or overhanging rock. The nest of the fork-tailed palm swift is fabricated of aglutinated feathers (of parrots, pigeons, etc.) snatched from the air or picked up from the ground by the swifts in full flight. It is affixed high inside a still-attached, drooping, dead frond of the Ité palm.

55 Family *Trogonidae*
TROGONS

The beautiful trogons are heavy, stout-bodied arboreal birds inhabiting heavily forested areas. Most occur in dense, wet rain forests; some prefer mixed bamboo jungle, others live in moist deciduous forests. All have large, dark eyes suitable for vision in the dim light of the jungle. They are loners, seldom seen even in pairs except at the nest, although one or two species are reported to occur in flocks.

In spite of being brilliantly colored, trogons are among the most difficult of forest birds to see when in repose. The underparts are, depending on the species, bright yellow, yellow-orange, scarlet or blood-red. These colors are unusually pure and intense. Even when detected they have an exasperating knack of always presenting their more sober-colored back to the viewer.

Usually one hears rather than sees a trogon. Their voices are muffled cooing, hooting, or hoarse, low barking sounds with a confusing ventriloquial quality.

Their food is taken largely on the wing — snapping insects like a flycatcher or picking berries while in hovering flight. A curious feature is that, in flight, their wings make a *frou-frou* sound like the rustling of taffeta.

The well-known quetzal, or resplendent trogon, is a member of this family. Although only the size of a magpie, its tail-coverts form a long, flowing train up to three feet in length and glitter like a hummingbird's. It is the national bird of Guatemala, symbolizing freedom — like the bald eagle of the United States. Its image is the central figure of the country's

162

Violaceous trogon

coat-of-arms and the *quetzal* is the monetary unit. The bird also appears on Guatemalan stamps and has graced both sides of its silver coinage since 1873.

Trogons are unique in that their yoked toes (two pointing forward and two backward) differ from all other yoke-toed birds. It is the inner front toe that is turned backward to join the hind toe, rather than the outer front toe, as is the case in parrots, cuckoos, owls, jacamars, puffbirds, barbets, toucans, woodpeckers, turacos, and honeyguides.

The name "trogon" comes from the Greek, a gnawer, alluding to the serrated or "toothed" edges of the upper mandible, a useful condition for gripping and crushing slippery, smooth fruit such as berries.

163

56 HUMMINGBIRDS

Family *Trochilidae*

Without regard to their technical characteristics, hummingbirds are known on sight by their diminutive size, glittering color, and their rapidly whirring, humming flight. They are more often confused with insects than with other birds; perhaps more accurately large sphinx moths when poised on misty pinions before a flower, long tongues extended into the semblance of a beak are often misidentified as crepuscular-flying hummers.

No other bird group possesses the singular powers of flight displayed by the *Trochilidae*. They are masters of controlled flight: forwards, hovering stationary with the body held vertically, and even backwards. Some species are capable of long sustained flight. The familiar ruby-throat is known to cross the Gulf of Mexico while on migration. Their amazing aerobatics are made possible by a short thick upper "arm" and a long, strong "wrist" and "hand." These are propelled by exceedingly powerful pectoral muscles which, in some species, make up one third of the bird's total weight. Another peculiarity of hummingbirds, which they share with woodpeckers, is that they are equipped with an extensile tongue with which they can extract nectar and small insects from deep-throated blossoms.

Perhaps the hummingbird's most noteworthy feature is its brilliant, prismatic color. Alas, many an observer in tropical America where most of the colorful species live has been perplexed and disappointed with the infrequency with which

Hummingbirds ▶

TaiShout.

Broad-tailed Hummingbird ♂
(Selasphorus platycercus)
Nualahuises, Nuevo Leon, Mexico
July 24, 1946.

Costa's Hummingbird ♂
Calypte costae
Ciudad Juarez, Mexico
Aug 1946

TaiShout.

Tufted Coquette. ♂
Lophornis ornata
Tacarigua, Trinidad
May 1957

TaiShout.

Lucifer Hummingbird ♂
(Calothorax lucifer)
Tepoztlan, Morelos, Mexico
Aug 7, 1946

Black-tailed trainbearer

these colors are visible. Because most of their splendor is the result of the diffraction of light through the feathers (whose basic pigments are black or dark brownish red), the viewer must be at precisely the right angle to both the bird and the light source to intercept it with his eye.

More than three hundred species have been identified and named. A few more are known only from millinery accessories from the days when they lavishly decorated women's hats.

57 KINGFISHERS

Family *Alcedinidae*

To describe the kingfishers from the New World species alone would be to give an erroneous or at best an imperfect idea of the family. To begin with, there are relatively few representatives of the group (about eight) in the Americas, while some forty or more kinds are known from the Australasian region and about a score from the warmer parts of Asia. Most species are tropical: only one resides in temperate Europe and one in temperate North America.

Despite the name king*fisher*, the majority of species are not piscivorous and are often found far from water within deep forests. These kinds, most of them small, feed on small lizards, large insects, and other invertebrates which they hunt in much the same way as some fish-eaters capture fish. That is, by dropping swiftly, beak first, from a vantage-perch on to ground-inhabiting prey.

The belted kingfisher of North America and the ringed kingfisher of Mexico south to Tierra del Fuego are among the giants of the family — big, rough-crested, boisterous birds found on non-polluted rivers, streams, and lakes. They dig nesting burrows of from two to fifteen feet long into vertical clay banks, laying the eggs at the enlarged extremity of the tunnel. (Forest species lay their eggs in a hole in a tree.) If there is no foothold on the bank at the point where the birds have decided to dig their tunnel (both male and female dig), they will fly repeatedly at the spot until they have dislodged enough earth with their dagger-like bills to provide one. Once the hole is started they dig with the beak, shovel the loose earth back

167

Belted Kingfisher ♀
Megaceryle alcyon
North Bay, Ontario
May, 1970

beneath them with their feet (which though small have the front toes fused together for part of their length), and finally push it out of the entrance hole with their tails. Dig, shovel, and sweep; a monumental achievement excavating a ten to fifteen-foot burrow.

Ringed kingfisher

It was formerly thought that kingfishers built nests of spotlessly cleansed fish bones in which to lay their eggs. Actually they build no nest at all other than a shallow saucer-shaped scrape at the terminus of the burrow. But kingfishers swallow their fishy foodstuffs whole and, unable to digest the bones, regurgitate them, thoroughly divested of all flesh and actually bleached by their stomach acids. Incubating birds disgorge while sitting on the eggs with the result that the eggs are ringed with a heap of fish bones.

◀ *Belted kingfisher*

58 MOTMOTS

Family *Momotidae*

Confined to the tropical New World with their headquarters in Central America, motmots are jay-sized birds predominantly colored in soft shades of green and usually with striking silvery-blue or turquoise-blue and black markings about the face. Some have the head and foreparts bright cinnamon.

The most interesting feature of motmots are the two much elongated central tail feathers — an example of the phenomenon known by the elephantine name of "aptosochromatism" which, broadly interpreted, means a change in the appearance of plumage without the loss or gain of feathers. In most cases it involves a line of weakness at some point along the barbs or even the shafts of feathers beyond which point the color of the feathers may differ from the basal portion. At a certain time of year the tips of the feathers break off sharply and cleanly at these boundaries, revealing the basal color of the feathers and giving the bird an entirely different appearance without moulting. Well-known examples of this phenomenon are the males of bobolinks and snow buntings. Both acquire the faultless black portions of their breeding dress by so shedding the long yellowish and brownish tips of the feathers which a week or so before had totally veiled the black. In the case of the snow bunting so much of the tip is shed that each feather is altered — from broadly rounded to sharply pointed.

Anyone living in the city may watch this process in action with the "bib" of the common house sparrow. All winter long the male's chin and throat are veiled with light grey, but in spring the tips providing the veiling drop off to disclose the black "bib" of the breeding dress.

Broad-billed motmot

In the motmots it is an area of about an inch to an inch and a half on either side of the shafts of the two greatly elongated central tail feathers that develops "fracture-points" at the base of the barbs. This portion of the vane of the feather breaks away, leaving a denuded shaft tipped by a broad, spatulate pendulum at the end. It was formerly thought that the motmot "in its vanity" plucked off these barbs to embellish its beauty, the notion having its origin in the fact that the bird's preening does help and hasten the process. The pendulum simile is all the more apt, as the perching motmot slowly swings its racquet-tipped tail back and forth sideways like the oscillating rod of a grandfather clock.

Of the eight species of motmots, two — the blue-crowned and the tody motmot — lack this peculiarity and retain complete long central tail feathers.

Malacoptila panamensis
Otovalo, Ecuador
May 1965

Whitewhiskered Puffbird
("Softwing")

59 PUFFBIRDS

Family *Bucconidae*

We think of warm-blooded birds as creatures of high metabolism and near constant animation. Indeed, this is generally true. A somewhat different situation exists in the heat and humidity of the tropical rain forest. The brightly colored birds of the leafy canopy, a hundred feet or more above the ground and drenched with blazing sunlight for most of the daylight hours, are vibrantly active and energetically vocal for brief periods following daybreak and before nightfall. During the hottest part of the day they become quiet and inactive.

But in the gloomy recesses of the forest interior lives another group of birds generally of modest color and different behavior. Shielded by the umbrella of the canopy from the direct scorching heat, they nevertheless must live in the enervating sultriness of the mid-levels of the jungle where light penetrates only feebly. These birds are prevailingly passive and lethargic, active in an apathetic way during most of the daylight hours. Among these are the thirty species of puffbirds, found only in the American tropics from southern Mexico to Ecuador and southern Brazil.

Puffbirds, so called from their habit of ruffling their feathers until they look half again as bulky, are stout, dumpy birds from six to ten inches long, with exceptionally large heads and bills. They sit quietly, bolt upright, occasionally darting out to snap up a lazily flying insect, sometimes returning to the same perch or more frequently to another of several vantage points used as lookouts for hunting. Such is the life of many of the birds of the understorey of the forest.

◄ *White-whiskered puffbird*

60 Family *Galbulidae*
JACAMARS

In the Old World there is a family of birds known as the bee-eaters: brightly plumaged, small to medium-sized birds that live on flying insects, have long pointed bills, short legs, and nest in earth tunnels burrowed into banks and shelving ground.

Although unrelated, the jacamars may be said to be the bee-eaters of the American tropics. Evolutionary processes have brought the two groups together in nearly every way: size, plumage, diet and feeding method, behavior, habitat, and nesting practice. Their everyday routine is almost identical yet differences of internal structure dictate that they be placed in separate orders: bee-eaters along with the kingfishers, motmots, and rollers; jacamars among the puffbirds, toucans, and woodpeckers.

Jacamars are mainly glittering green in color, the brilliance of their iridescence rivalling and even transcending that of the sparkling hummingbirds. Jacamars sit patiently on favorite perches in savanna woodland or about the edges of a forest — bill held upward at a 30 to 45-degree angle until a flying insect appears. Then they dart after it in dashing, swooping flight. Like the larger tyrant flycatchers, puffbirds, and motmots, they flail large strong insects like cicadas, beetles, locusts, and mantids against the bark of tree limbs until they are killed or rendered inert before swallowing them, often breaking off hard, horny parts such as grasshopper legs or the wing-cases of beetles. It is an act of such violence as to make an observer flinch.

Many of their sallies after airborne insects carry them straight up for forty or more feet and the celerity with which they snap fast-moving targets out of the air is made all the more extraordinary when one considers how seemingly ill-fitted the long, thin forceps-like beak is for the task. Most other flycatching groups of birds have broad flat beaks or wide cavernous mouths. Yet those who have seen jacamars in action agree that they are the most expert of all.

Rufous-tailed jacamar

I once watched a jacamar darting repeatedly into a large assemblage of *Heliconius* butterflies that had been attracted to a wet spot on a jungle track. One at a time it picked them off, returning to its perch after each capture to rub off the wings before eating the body.

Sulphurbreasted Toucan

Ramphastos sulphuratus

Acatlan, Puebla, Mexico
Aug. 1946

61 Family *Ramphastidae*
TOUCANS

The fantastically large colorful beaks of the toucans have made
them famous, notorious, and the jestingstock of cartoonists.
They are made sport of as "banana-beaks" and indeed the
beaks of some of the larger species do resemble the shape and
color of bananas. The beak of the toco toucan, six inches in
length, is orange-yellow like a very ripe banana and comes
complete with a black (overripe) spot near the tip. That of the
keel-billed toucan is red and green, similar to an unripe but
ripening red banana. Cuvier's toucan's beak is black like a
banana long gone. Others resemble in varying degrees
bananas in varying stages. The huge beaks appear
cumbersome but in fact are almost as light as a feather owing
to their hollow interior strengthened by a cellular network of
air chambers, like hardened foam plastic.

Not only the beak is remarkable. Among other
peculiarities is the ownership of *blue* flesh, as well as a singular
pterylography — feathers implanted all over the body instead
of in orderly tracts with naked spaces in between as in most
other birds.

Toucans have a graceful undulating flight that can be
silent or, as they will, make a great rushing sound. They climb
and hop from branch to branch with great dexterity and their
loud croaks, nasal barking and screeching, scratching notes are
characteristic sounds of the rain forest. They are playful birds
and two or more will spar and tussle with their gigantic beaks
— a truly comical sight.

◀ *Keel-billed toucan*

Sulphur-and-white-breasted toucan in Monstera

As an encore to the endowments of the toucans, we can add that in sleeping the toucan turns its head, lays the great length of the beak along the center of the back, and then cocks up its tail until it envelops the beak like a coverlet. It puts its beak to bed!

The name toucan comes from the Amerindian name *tucan* for the bird in Brazil. These people considered barbecued toucan a delicacy. Explorers who have eaten toucan agree, blue flesh and all.

178

62 WOODPECKERS

Family *Picidae*

Tail feathers rigid and pointed; bill a chisel. This description will serve for the recognition of any of the true woodpeckers if, indeed, one is needed. Most people are familiar with the industrious, myopic birds that cling to the vertical boles and branches of trees and hitch themselves upward, audibly pecking away at the bark in search of insects' larvae.

Woodpeckers are found throughout the world (except in Australasia, Madagascar, and some of the oceanic islands) wherever there are trees or where cacti take the place of trees in desert regions. South America is richest in kinds, with many strikingly beautifully colored species. Many have big, erect and pointed, ostentatious crests which, combined with their alert, joggily, jouncy movements, give them an impressive appearance.

The tongues of woodpeckers are without parallel in birds. The hyoid bones (the skeleton of the tongue) are extraordinarily elongated, curling up over the back of the skull and forward over the cranium; in some species continuing until they reach around the orbit of the right eye; in others running into the right nostril at the base of the beak. These long, thin rods of bone are enwrapped in highly developed elastic muscles by means of which the birds can thrust out the tongue to several inches beyond the tip of the bill. Watch a flicker licking up ants from an anthill (for this is a woodpecker that spends much of its time on the ground and is a familiar sight on suburban lawns). It seems to sit motionless, but all the while it is probing its long tongue into the ants' ground tunnels; adult ants, eggs, and larvae adhere to this organ because of the glutinous saliva that coats it. They are drawn into the mouth and swallowed. Other kinds of woodpeckers that excavate into infected trees for wood-boring beetle larvae have the extensile tongue equipped with barbs on which the grubs are impaled for extraction and devoured. Some, like the sapsuckers, have a brush-like tip to the tongue for lapping up the sweet juices of trees which they tap in the same way we do for maple sugar.

Yellow-shafted flicker

Woodpeckers normally have four toes: two directed forward, one backward, and one reversible. The last can be directed forward, sideways, or backward as the conformation of the bird's perpendicular or sloping perch dictates. A few kinds have only three toes which are usually carried in an open Y position in climbing.

Pileated woodpecker ▶

Pileated Woodpecker ♂
<u>Dryocopus</u> <u>pileatus</u>.
July 28, 1947
Malachi, Kenora Dist. Ontario

63 Family *Capitonidae*
BARBETS

These are small to medium-sized, stout-bodied, large-headed birds with a toe arrangement similar to that of puffbirds and woodpeckers; that is, two pointing forward and two backward. Some species climb and feed like woodpeckers, but their tails are not stiff and rather than chiseling into wood they confine themselves largely to prising and tearing away bits of loose bark in search of insects and spiders. Most kinds are also fruit-eaters and their bills are dentate; that is, with tooth-like notches on the cutting edges. These serrations presumably are an aid in plucking and manipulating fruits.

The name "barbet" was given them because of the long bristles that project from the chin and around the gape. Only recently it has been discovered that these bristles have a droll but very real function. Normally spread out fanwise, on either side of the bill and mouth, they can be drawn in until they lie flat along the bill. They actually perform as sensory organs and are used to calibrate the size of berries and other fruit! As a berry is gripped between the mandibles, the long whiskers depress and come into contact with the fruit, measuring its dimensions as if the whiskers were many-digited calipers. Berries over a certain size are rejected; the smaller ones are accepted and eaten. This prevents the bird from attempting to swallow berries that are too bulky for its gullet and choking on them.

The plumage of barbets is colorful and variegated; in some kinds even gaudy. Many have patches of bright reds, blues, greens, and yellows. The feathers are hard-surfaced with a

182

pronounced sheen which accentuates their brilliance. The wings are short and rounded and seem adequate only for short flights. Some species, if danger threatens while they are perched high up, drop like stones until near the ground, then level and fly off a few feet above the surface.

Red-headed barbet

Of the approximately seventy-five world species, more than half live in Africa, about two dozen in Asia, and a dozen in tropical America.

The South American species are rather silent and solitary but sometimes join foraging parties of tanagers, wood warblers, shrike vireos, antbirds, and others. These hunting flocks of mixed tree-inhabiting species are a phenomenon of the tropics; encountered in temperate regions only in fortuitous aggregations during the migration seasons or in winter bands of a few chickadees, a nuthatch or two, a tree creeper, and perhaps one or two downy or hairy woodpeckers.

Cocoa Woodcreeper ♂
Xiphorhynchus guttatus
Mt. El Tucuché, Trinidad
May, 1957

T.M.Shortt

64

Family *Dendrocolaptidae*

WOODCREEPERS

About fifty species have been recognized of this rather uniform Neotropical family. Those familiar with the North American and European tree creeper (brown creeper), on making first acquaintance with a member of the *Dendrocolaptidae* will hardly believe that they are unrelated. Although most kinds are considerably larger than the tree creeper, they have a similar slender conformation, stiffened tail feathers, short, powerful, climbing feet and claws, and brown, rufous, and olivaceous coloring. Their habit is identical: starting near the base of a tree they spiral upward until the trunk has been inspected for insects and their eggs and larvae, as well as spiders, mites, and other small invertebrates which shelter in and under the bark; then they fly with a nearly closed-wing glide to the base of another tree and repeat the routine.

Woodcreepers occur (in different species) in nearly every type of tropical woodland: dense rain forest, mangrove swamps, cocoa and coconut plantations, bamboo groves, and at all levels from lowland to mountain forests. Some have the beak very much as in the tree creeper, others have long straight, long sickle-shaped, short awl-shaped, or stout upturned wedge-like beaks; each is ideally suited for probing and picking according to vegetation and the nature of the preferred prey.

Woodcreepers are for the most part solitary birds. They range from Sonora in northwestern Mexico to Argentina,

◄ *Cocoa woodcreeper*

185

Bolivia, and Peru. They occur also in Trinidad and Tobago. Very little is known about the nesting habits of most kinds, but some have been recorded as using natural cavities in trees or abandoned woodpecker nesting-holes, which they then re-line. The eggs, like those of most cavity or burrow-nesting birds, are white.

Spot-crowned woodcreeper

One may see several of the same or different species together when they join the mixed gatherings of antbirds, tyrant flycatchers, ovenbirds, and other kinds attracted by columns of army ants on the march. All feed on the insects that have been stirred up by the ants and which are running or flying to escape. They even feed upon the ants themselves.

65 ANTBIRDS

Family *Formicariidae*

The antbirds were so christened because many of the 220 different species follow columns of army ants when the latter move from one bivouac to another. Those who have seen the hordes of other insects: spiders, centipedes, millipedes, slugs, and other small creatures routed out of their homes and hiding places to flee the merciless onslaught of the ants will understand their attraction for insectivorous birds. The ants literally act as beaters, driving the weaker animals into the waiting gapes of the birds.

Some species of antbirds even have calls that are used exclusively while following ants. These notes, recognized by others of their own kind and by different species as well, alert them to the fortuitous feast; a curious summoning of competitors by birds that are normally somewhat solitary. It is useful to learn the "ant-call" of these birds, for the naturalist hearing the *chirr* of the barred bush-strike, for example, can retreat before being painfully bitten by the ants or, he can, if courageous, advance in the certainty that he will find a host of several species of ant-following birds that otherwise might be extremely difficult to encounter.

The great majority of antbirds are denizens of the ground or of the gloomy understorey of the rain forest, but some species also occur in secondary forests, around plantations, and even in home gardens. There is such great diversity of form, bill shape, color, and tail length among the various species that different groups within the family have been called ant-shrikes, ant-thrushes, ant-wrens, ant-pittas, and

Whitebarred Bush-Shrike ♂
Thamnophilus doliatus fraterculus
Mt Aripo Trinidad, May 1957

TMShortt

ant-vireos. These names are suggestive of their appearance, behavior, or both, but coining such names should be discouraged — they are not shrikes, wrens, or vireos, nor are they even related to them.

Great ant shrike, ant pitta, barred bush-shrike

Some antbirds are decorated with baroque crests and tufts of feathers. The barred bush-shrike has a long, shaggy crest that flops in an unruly manner; the white-plumed antbird has most novel "horns" formed of thick tufts of pure white feathers which rise to a point on either side of the head from in front of the eyes and a short white goatee. This species is the most consistently ant-following of the family. Flocks of up to three dozen accumulate about a single ant column. Other antbirds, such as the ocellated antbird and the bare-eye, have large, naked patches about the eyes which are highly colored in blue or rosy red.

◄　*Barred bush-shrike*

189

66 OVENBIRDS

Family *Furnariidae*

It is unfortunate that one of the best known of the North American wood warblers should have been given the name of ovenbird, causing confusion with this huge assemblage of well over two hundred species (one of the larger bird families) which in itself perhaps could have had a more all-inclusive name, since relatively few of them build oven-shaped nests. The real "ovenbird" is a common species in Argentina, Brazil, and Paraguay and is called the red ovenbird or in Spanish *El Hornero*, "the baker." It builds, often on projecting parts of houses such as cornices or even on the roof, a large mud nest which, with the entrance on the side, bears a strong resemblance to an old-fashioned oven or kiln.

But the red ovenbird is not typical of the majority of ovenbirds. An idea of their versatility can be gained by a perusal of some of the names given to various groups within the family: spinetails, tree-runners, house-keepers, miners, plains-runners, earth-creepers, shake-tails, tree-hunters, foliage-gleaners, leaf-scrapers, and stream-creepers; most of them atrocious names but with the small virtue of at least giving some concept of the enormous variety of adaptations and behavior for which this group is renowned.

Their nests exhibit a heterogeneity that is almost unbelievable: they range from neat, cup-like birds' nests to the great barrel-like piles of several kinds of cachalotes (Spanish: cah-chah-loh-tay — the sperm whale — but why?) Built of sticks up to two feet in length, these nests may be as much as four feet across with a small entrance hole in one side that opens into a chamber ample enough for a turkey to sit in!

Some of the spinetails build a long tube-like passageway to the entrance hole on the side of their bulky nests, which is formed entirely by the interlocking of thorny twigs and has an outside diameter of about four inches. Its interior, bristling

Streaked xenops

with needle-sharp thorns, is wide enough only to allow the birds to pick their way through it, to and from the nest. The firewood-gatherer builds its nest high up in a tall tree; a nest a foot in diameter and two feet high. The entrance is at the top and access to the egg-chamber at the bottom is by a spiral shaft-like corridor. The birds are not very adroit at weaving the sticks into the structure, and so many fall to the ground beneath the nesting tree that they were given the name of "firewood-gatherers."

Although so versatile in their ecology, the ovenbirds' plumage color is predominantly brown — a drab-looking dress for birds of such exciting behavior.

67 Family *Tyrannidae*
TYRANT FLYCATCHERS

North America is well stocked with tyrant flycatchers. It is home to about three dozen species, some of which, in good numbers, occur northward to the limit of trees. In fact, this represents only the tip of the iceberg, as well over three hundred additional kinds inhabit Latin America south of the Rio Grande.

The tyrants are a uniform group, showing nothing like the variety of that other large New World family, the ovenbirds. Most of them are rather small greenish-olive birds with short, rounded crests. Most exhibit the same erect perching posture and the same custom of flitting up after passing insects.

But even among the regimental tyrants, nature's propensity for experimentation emerges sporadically. The little royal flycatcher of Mexico to Brazil has its head adorned with the most flamboyant crest of all passerine birds, with the possible exception of the King of Saxony bird of paradise. When erected the royal flycatcher's crest is fan-shaped like the tail of a peacock and is a fiery, coppery red, each feather tipped with lustrous blue-black and pale grey. Regrettably, the crest is seldom raised and normally lies flattened on the crown. It is likely that many observers, seeing the otherwise drab little bird in the dim light of the lower levels of the rain forest, have disregarded it as just another "little brown job."

Those familiar with the south-central United States will have seen the handsome scissor-tailed flycatcher, a kingbird-sized flycatcher delicately colored in hoary-ash and

Western kingbird ▶

Immature ♂
(Arkansas
Kingbird.)

Western Kingbird
Tyrannus verticalis

Deer Lodge, Man.
Aug 16 1930

Inside
mouth
Principally
orange-yellow
some fleshy
at tongue
2 spots pale
blue on roof

Feet are
dark slate-grey
light lines.
claws very
dark grey

T.M.Shortt.

salmon-pink and furnished with outer tail feathers ten inches in length. Its close relative, the fork-tailed flycatcher, is of more southerly distribution. Visitors to Trinidad or Tobago in the summer months may see large migrant flocks of these beautiful flycatchers.

Fork-tailed flycatcher

In the cock-tailed tyrant the two outer tail feathers have broad, coarse webs which are carried vertically, giving the bird in flight the appearance of an aircraft with twin tail-fins. Even more curious is the strange-tailed tyrant—a feeble flying bird, the outer tail feathers of which are ten inches long.

194

68 Family *Cotingidae*
COTINGAS

The cotingas are another exclusively New World family comprising just under one hundred species which range in size from little more than three inches to almost two feet in length. They exhibit some of the most bizarre ornamental appendages and uncommon pigmentation to be found in the vast avian assortment. Particularly unusual are bright opaque cerulean blue, red-violet, rich purple, scarlet, and brilliant orange. What makes these colors doubly glamorous is that they are pigment colors rather than structural ones (like those of jacamars and hummingbirds) and do not depend on the viewer being at the correct angle to catch the refractive facets but retain their brilliance regardless of aspect.

Few birds can match the big umbrellabirds for grotesque adornment. Black, crow-sized birds, they have huge crests which, when erected, fan out like a parasol or a mushroom and cover the whole head and beak under a canopy. They also have an inflatable flap or lappet which hangs from the throat. In one species this feathered pendant is over a foot long, as long as the bird's body. In another it is bright red and unfeathered.

One segment of the family comprises the four jay-sized bellbirds renowned for their loud ringing cries (although one *moos* like a cow). One species found in Venezuela and Trinidad is known as the anvil bird or *El Campanero*, the bell-ringer. Its cries are indeed like the clang of steel on an anvil. The *mooing* bellbird, aptly named the calfbird, is, along with some other cotingas, peculiar among song birds in that the polygamous males take no part in the nesting chores but spend morning

ANVIL BIRD ♂
Procnias averant

Hollis Reservoir,
   Northern Range, Trinidad
      May 1957 -

T.M.Shell

and evening sessions in display areas, their behavior there being similar in its biological implications to that of some species of grouse at their leks or communal dancing grounds.

Black-tailed tityra

Several dominant males occupy individual prominent lek perches and go through stylized ritual posturing with much *mooing*, while immature or subservient males sit on lower and less prominent perches, also performing. When an observer captures one of the dominant males for banding and photography, then releases him, the bird is nervous and exhausted, with the result that he loses his dominance and his prime lek perch to another bird.

This is only one example of many that should be a warning to biologists who "study behavior" of birds in the wild by attaching plastic streamers, radio transmitters, and other paraphernalia to their subjects, or, dye parts of them pink or blue or purple. The results so obtained are highly suspect and should not be accepted dogmatically as representing normal conduct.

◄ *Anvil bird*

197

69 TAPACULOS

Family *Rhinocryptidae*

Tapaculo, the Spanish-American name for these birds is derived from *tapar*, to cover and *culo*, behind or bottom. Its insinuation is "cover your bottom," a witty and congruous name for the tiny birds that run with their tails in the air, exposing their posteriors. Would we could say as much for their scientific family name, *Rhinocryptidae* which means "hidden nose" and so is another nonsense name. The nomenclator possibly was trying to refer to a more or less concealed movable covering for the nostrils, an appendage designed to prevent dust from entering the lungs in their windswept habitat. In Argentina they are called *gallito* or "little cock" for indeed they have the perky aplomb of game cocks.

The twenty-seven tapaculos are all terrestrial birds of the grasslands, semi-desert scrub, or the high forests of South America. They are past masters in the art of skulking but also, like wrens, obsessed with curiosity and frequently dart out of hiding places for a momentary appraisal of anything alien. Few other birds can run like tapaculos. Size for size they outstrip even ostriches and roadrunners — not with the dainty, mincing run of most passerine birds but with a nimble-stepping sprint with strides of six inches and even more; greater than their own total length, including tail! I once startled an ocellated tapaculo at the edge of a jungle trail and for a moment thought the scurrying thing was some sort of fleet-footed rodent. Then it turned across the trail, stopped with its tail cocked well over its back, studied me for about one second, and then tore into the jungle on the opposite side. The whole episode lasted less than five seconds.

198

The plumage of tapaculos is lax and fluffy, especially around that exposed bottom; their wings are short, weak, and very nearly useless. With their speed afoot flight is unnecessary in their chosen environment, well supplied with protective shelter. In dissecting a tapaculo one is instantly impressed by the thick, hard, well-developed muscles of the leg and thigh and by the soft flabbiness of the pectorals which supply the motive power for flight.

Ocellated tapaculo

Tapaculos are insectivorous and scratch like barnyard fowl among the debris on the ground or the forest floor to uncover delicacies such as spiders, caterpillars, millipedes, and other small creatures.

Their songs are for the most part raspy clucks and cackles which probably contribute in part to the *gallito* image.

HORNED LARK   ad ♂
(Otocoris a. alpestris)
LAKE HARBOUR, BAFFIN ISLAND.
JULY 20 1938.

T.M.Shortt

70 LARKS

Family *Alaudidae*

The larks are mainly an African family: nearly fifty of the seventy-five world species occur there. Eleven are found in Europe but only one, the horned lark, has pioneered into the New World.

The American representative, the horned lark, is one of the widest ranging of all song birds. Its home territory in the Americas is from northern Alaska, Prince Patrick, and Devon Islands in the Canadian high arctic, south to southern Mexico and with a sequestered population in the savannas at high altitudes in the Colombian Andes.

It was like meeting old friends to encounter horned larks high above Darjeeling where they frequent alpine meadows and gravelly screes. One of the Mount Everest expeditions found horned larks feeding at refuse heaps at every Tibetan village in the high plateaus. The larks also visited the explorers' camp at 16,500 feet. It is no less remarkable to find these fragile-looking birds on the windswept semi-barrens of Somerset and Devon Islands in the Canadian arctic, feeding nonchalantly among stranded icebergs along the coast or in the vicinity of vast patches of permanent snow.

Wherever one encounters this bird, its bright, tinkly melody is the same. Delivered either from a low prominence such as a small boulder or while performing bounding and fluttering aerial exercises, the song resembles the tiny bell sounds of hanging wind chimes stirred by a gentle breeze.

◄ *Horned lark*

71 Family *Pipridae* MANAKINS

Pipridae is derived from the Greek *pipra*, a woodpecker, and is a ridiculous malapropism. Neither in appearance nor habit do manakins resemble woodpeckers.

Manakins are brightly colored, intensely active, tiny birds, most no more than four or five inches in length. They frequent many of the tropical and subtropical forests of the New World.

The naturalist who has become exasperated trying to observe either the shy, retiring terrestrial birds or the foliage-concealed denizens of the canopy of the tropical rain forest, is grateful for these tame, conspicuous, and entertaining little gnomes. Their eyes, with white, pale yellow or sometimes red irises, are large, bright, darting, and alive. From a distance of a few feet one may even watch their spectacular courtship performances, with the actors paying no more attention to their audience than human players on the legitimate stage.

The stages for manakin histrionics vary with the particular species, but within a given species they are consistent. The blue-backed manakin chooses a horizontal perch two to three feet above the forest floor. Two males engage in the dance which consists of jumping again and again over each other's backs. When one jumps, the other shuffles quickly along the branch to occupy the exact position vacated by the jumper. Then *it* jumps and the first jumper now scurries sidelong to the "take-off" spot. This may be repeated dozens of times. If a person draws a half-circle, open end down, and, continuing the stroke, closes it with a horizontal "equator" line he will have indicated the movement enacted alternately by the birds.

While in the air the birds make a quick series of rasping sounds that can be approximated by scraping a thumbnail along the teeth of a comb. This is made by flipping the stiff wing feathers against each other on the principle of snapping one's fingers.

Blue-backed manakin

Each of the five dozen species of manakins has its own special courtship dance. The dance is accompanied by a variety of vocal and wing-made mechanical sounds, but all fall within the same genre. The black-and-white manakin, from a perch about eighteen inches from the ground, flies in a straight line past the perched female. As he passes he makes a sharp cracking sound like the report of a cap-gun and buzzing sounds which are probably vocal.

After mating, female manakins go off and build frail little basket-like nests in which they deposit two or three eggs and do all the work of hatching and rearing the young. The polygamous males, meanwhile, continue their activities "on stage," each presumably serving as many hens as he can attract with his pop-gun.

72 SWALLOWS

Family *Hirundinidae*

As a family the swallows have adjusted to a harmonious existence with the human race to a degree unequalled by other bird groups. Barn swallows and cliff swallows find the overhanging eaves of man's edifices eminently suited to their nesting requirements. His cattle, pigs, and other domesticated animals ensure an ample supply of flying insects around the nesting sites, and his artificial ponds supply drinking water. The soft-earth-burrowing bank and rough-winged swallows, formerly dependent on steep river banks and other such natural phenomena, have found in the cut-banks for railway lines and highways a bonanza of nesting situations. Tree swallows happily expropriate hollows in fence posts in which to raise their young.

Humans, appreciating their swift-flying, cheerful presence and insect-catching propensities, reciprocate by providing nesting boxes for them. These are eagerly accepted by tree swallows and particularly by the large, steely-blue purple martins, colonies of which take over man-made "apartment houses" which, erected on long poles, become landmarks in some communities. I have been directed by a farmer to the "third house past the big martin colony near the center of town."

Several tropical American species such as the black-capped swallow and the grey-breasted martin also make use of human structures, but some prefer old mud nests of ovenbirds. Other kinds of swallows have remained indifferent to the human invasion and have retained their aboriginal nesting customs. Among these are the violet-green swallow of the Pacific coast from Alaska to Mexico and thence southward on the great Mexican plateau. They still prefer natural cliffs and rock faces. Another is the mangrove swallow of Mexico to Panama and Peru which remains formal in its choice of the natural banks of streams and rivers.

Almost every activity of swallows — feeding, drinking, migrating, playing, even scratching and preening — is performed on the wing. Early writers claimed that they even mate while in flight (not true!). Such aerially adapted birds are naturally well versed in the vagaries of air pressures and air currents, but it is their flying insect prey that determine the altitudes at which we see them. Rising air lifts insects to higher levels and consequently swallows follow them. This is why we often see swallows flying high before storms or sometimes immediately after them.

Mangrove swallow

73 Family *Motacillidae*
PIPITS and WAGTAILS

Most of the fifty odd species of these terrestrial, sparrow-sized birds are adapted to life in open habitats — arctic tundra, prairie grassland, mountain meadows, and sparsely vegetated scrub lands.

They are slender birds with dainty feet. The family divides easily into two branches — one, the wagtails, which unfortunately have penetrated the New World only as tenuously established colonists from Asia into northern and western Alaska. Two species of these confiding and attractive birds, the yellow wagtail and the pied wagtail may, in the distant future, expand from their as yet insecure foothold in America and add another charming element to our avifauna; two, the pipits, which are also essentially birds of the Old World. Only two kinds have firmly established themselves in North America, although a third, the petchora pipit, has bred in western Alaska.

Sprague's pipit nests only in the central prairies, preferring the long-grass prairie — the mother country of its confreres, the long-billed curlew, the marbled godwit, and the upland plover. It is also the habitat of the prairie chicken, western meadowlark, and Baird's sparrow. Here, in a land of distant horizons and large, lucent skies, this pipit mounts so high in the air as to become an almost invisible speck. There it pours out its love song. Flying in wide circles it repeats over and over, in a thin, sweet voice, a silvery, spiraling melody. It is sung in a steadily descending scale, lasts five or six seconds, drops a full octave between the first high note and the last, and may be repeated scores of times in one session aloft. Its melody is reminiscent of that of the forest-dwelling thrush, the veery. But it has the ringing quality of fine crystal rather than the golden tone of the thrush and seems entirely in harmony with the bright vastness of its theatre. It has been one of my favorite bird voices since boyhood, but admittedly there is partiality involved; nostalgia mingles with my enjoyment and touches chords that may not be stirred by other equally romantic sights and sounds.

Sprague's pipit

At the conclusion of Sprague's pipit's flight-song cycle, it drops like a stone on closed wings into the long grass and becomes one of the most difficult of all prairie birds to spot.

The other American pipit is the water pipit, a circumpolar species whose name is not entirely appropriate, for it is essentially a bird of the grassy mountain plateaus and the arctic tundra. It, too, performs a song-flight, but at considerably lower levels than Sprague's pipit and its tinkly song is thin and short.

74 Family *Laniidae*
SHRIKES

Shrikes are another essentially Old World family with seventy-one of the seventy-three world species living exclusively in the eastern hemisphere. One, the great grey shrike, is holarctic in distribution. Another, the loggerhead shrike, is confined to North America.

Naturalists from the New World, familiar only with the grey, white, and black coloration of the two American species who visit Africa for the first time, are amazed at the variety of color and habitat of the many shrikes there. Reds and yellows and greens are common among the bush-shrikes which may be encountered either in dry thornbrush country or in the dense undergrowth of lush forests. Other kinds are pinkish-brown; magpie-like black-and-white patterns are also common.

The colloquial name of "butcher-bird" is a fitting one, for shrikes are indeed "song-birds-of-prey." Unlike other predatory birds, they kill with their strongly hooked beaks rather than with talons. The feet, although stout and used to carry larger items of prey such as mice and small birds, are as ill-equipped for killing as those of other song birds. Part of the "butcher" image comes from their custom of stockpiling food items by impaling victims on the spines of one or more selected thornbushes or hanging them between forks of twigs. An examination of a shrike's favored bush will often reveal a mouse, a small bird, and perhaps three or four large grasshoppers skewered or hung as if in a meat market.

Great grey shrike ▶

Great Gray Shrike ♂
Lanius excubitor
Ahmik L., Parry Sound, Ont.
Jan 10, 1967

My admiration for the great grey shrike was enhanced when, on a collecting trip to the Yukon, I found in a "larder" a rare species of mouse, fresh and virtually undamaged (save that it had been killed), that was high on my list of desiderata but which all my ingenuity had failed to uncover. I hated to steal it but convinced myself that such a skillful hunter would no doubt easily capture more. With this in mind I went back several times at daily intervals, but found only common field mice!

Migrant shrike

Shrikes are conspicuous birds and rest on prominently exposed perches. They fly strongly in a gently undulating fashion, usually close to the ground; they rise to their chosen perch with a very characteristic and dramatic upward sweep.

That they are true song birds is demonstrated by the lengthy warbling song of the great grey shrike. It is reminiscent of some of the finer phrases of the song of the catbird, and rates as one of the superior bird songs when measured by human yardsticks.

75 Family *Bombycillidae*
WAXWINGS and SILKY FLYCATCHERS

The family name of this somewhat catch-all group means "silky," a most fitting name and one that pinpoints the main external feature that binds together the three species of waxwings, the four kinds of silky flycatchers, and the strange, aberrant, white-winged *Hypocolius* that is isolated in the valley of the Tigris and Euphrates rivers in Iraq.

The waxwings are so called because of the singular extension of the shafts of the inner secondary feathers of the wing into flattened tear-drop-shaped scarlet processes that have almost the exact color and texture of old-fashioned sealing-wax. One of the three waxwings, the Japanese waxwing, does not develop these waxy extensions (it is a non-wax-wing!).

The two species which are common in parts of North America are the cedar waxwing, which nests northward almost to the limit of trees and southward to the southern tier of states of the United States, and the Bohemian waxwing, which also occurs in northern Europe and Asia, and is confined largely to the northwest from the mouth of the Mackenzie River to Idaho and Montana. These birds might have pleased the lisping king of Spain with their immaculate dress, gentle, polite manners, and their soft, sibilant voices — polite because a common habit is for one bird of a flock to delicately offer a berry to another, who in turn passes it to a third. As many as six or eight birds may engage in this food-passing, and the berry may travel up and down the line several times before one finally swallows the by now somewhat sodden fruit.

TMShortt

Bohemian Waxwing juv ♂
(Bombycilla g. pallidiceps)
Dezadeash Lake, Yukon
Aug. 9. 1944.

In addition to the "sealing-wax" decorations, American waxwings have fine upstanding crests, black robbers' face masks, and bright yellow tips to the tail feathers. The Japanese waxwing differs in having the tip of the tail light red, as if it had been dipped in red ink.

Grey silky flycatcher

My first exposure to this species was with skins in the research collection of the Royal Ontario Museum and I had grave misgivings that the specimens had been tampered with — that someone was perpetrating a hoax, especially since their data labels, in Japanese characters, were written in red ink of identically the same shade! I harbored lingering suspicions until, many years later, I encountered a flock of free, wild waxwings in Japan. Their tail-tips *were* red!

The silky flycatchers are of even more slender build than the waxwings but resemble them in having smooth, soft silky feathers, prominent crests, and the same fruit-eating habit.

◀ *Bohemian waxwing*

76 Family *Cinclidae*
DIPPERS

American dipper

The dipper was known to the ancient Greeks who, naturally, had a word for it: *Kinklos* from which we get the family name *Cinclidae*.

The four species of dippers are all of a size and differ only with respect to color details. The white-headed dipper frequents mountain streams of the Andes from Colombia to Argentina. The white-breasted dipper lives in similar habitat from Scandinavia to northwest Africa and eastward to and including the Himalayan Alps. In the Himalayas it coexists with the brown dipper — a rather anomalous situation where two very closely allied species of the same size, habit, and annual routine live side by side on the same stream. The fourth dipper is the North American or grey dipper of the western mountains from Alaska to Panama.

All are inhabitants of swift-running torrents, preferring the vicinity of rapids. Where glacial waters plunge through forests, rushing under ice-bridges, and dashing against boulders in showers of spume and spray, the dipper flits and perches on slippery rocks in mid-stream, cocking its stubby tail and bobbing its head. It plunges into the water in search of aquatic insect larvae and may remain beneath the surface for quite half a minute, *walking* freely on the stream bottom. It does not grip the stones with its feet, but keeps submerged by the simple expedient of tilting its body to an angle at which the force of the current is sufficient to keep it pressed down (a sort of reverse principle to that of air movement keeping a kite *up*). It is a more difficult feat, perhaps, than walking on the water like jaçanas.

More remarkable still, for a small song bird, it can and does fly underwater with its wings. When the dipper surfaces, it springs on to a stone, shakes the water off its greasy plumage (which has a distinctive musty, wren-like smell), bobs a few times, and bursts into a rollicking wren-like song: a suitable accompaniment to the roar of the white water.

One goes away marvelling at the starling-sized bird, unbelievably hardy, indifferent to cold and noise and wet, eternally hyper-kinetic, and frequently erupting with joyous, bubbling song — all this with no highly specialized morphological structure to do it with except an operculum to close the nostrils, a highly developed third eyelid or nictitating membrane, and an oil gland at the base of the tail at least ten times the size of that of other birds.

77 Family *Troglodytidae*
WRENS

This family reverses the circumstances of the larks, only one of which infiltrated into America. So, while the Americas abound with sixty kinds of wrens, only one, the beloved "Jenny" wren of England, is found in the eastern hemisphere. Strangely enough, the "Jenny" wren, which ranges from Iceland, through all Europe, and across Asia to Japan, Sakhalin and the Kuriles, is known throughout Europe as a familiar, confiding bird about human dwellings; in North America it is a retiring little skulker of the remote wilderness forests (the winter wren), and its place around buildings and in man's affection is taken by an entirely different species — the endemic house wren, a slightly larger and even more ebullient bird than the "Jenny."

The differences in the behavior of the two winter "Jenny" wren populations — European and American — even extend to their voices. The Old World birds sing a prolonged, strident jumble of trills and jingles which may last as long as five seconds; but listen to the American bird in the dark recesses of the cedar swamp or black spruce bog. From a moss-covered stump or a miniature cave under the roots of a fallen tree emanates a quiet rippling cadence that gradually swells and grows into a ringing, rolling barrage of hurried song. I have timed some that rattled merrily on for a full ten seconds, the longest single song of any bird of my experience.

Some of the American wrens have adjusted to marsh situations: the marsh wren in the cattails over standing water,

Carolina wren ▶

T.M.Shortt

Carolina Wren. ♂
(Thryothorus ludovicianus.)
Point Pelee. Ont
May 13, 1941.

the sedge wrens in wet, grassy flatlands. Others have occupied the deserts, nesting in cholla, yucca, or thorny mesquite. One lives on the sandstone ledges of towering cliffs, rocky mesas, and deep canyons — the canyon wren, and cowboys have nicknamed it the "scale-bird" for its clear liquid notes drop down the chromatic scale.

Grey-barred wren

Others prefer the oak and pine forests of the high Mexican plateau; some live in the undergrowth of the humid tropical rain forests; others even in the moss, lichen, and epiphyte-bedecked high-altitude cloud forests. In the Americas wrens are everywhere, but most kinds prefer the tangled edges of woodlands and thickets — in fact, anything that resembles a brushpile to lurk in.

Some are even smaller than the winter wren, others larger than a thrush, but whichever the species and wherever they live, the wren character prevails: effervescent, vocal, and full of verve. They even sing in the face of an enemy, such as a rattlesnake or a weasel — "the happy warriors!"

78 Family *Mimidae*
MOCKINGBIRDS and THRASHERS

The outstanding characteristic of this family is its merit as a group of songsters.

Mimidae are strictly New World, with their center of abundance both of species and individuals in the warm, arid southwestern United States and Mexico. Eighteen of the thirty-one species are found in Mexico.

Many kinds of birds practice mimicry — starlings, parrots, leaf birds, and others — but the efforts of most are, to the practiced ear, obviously counterfeit. Not so with the northern mockingbird. Its fame both as a singer and impersonator is justly earned. Many birds *imitate* the songs of other species; the mockingbird *sings* them.

The most dramatic proof of this came when mockingbirds picked up the song of caged nightingales at the Bok Singing Tower in Florida. Sound spectrographs taken of the mockingbirds' rendition show them to be exact duplicates, even to the high-pitched overtones that are beyond the capacity of the human ear to hear. The northern mockingbird copies more than just bird sounds. It does equally well with a sewing machine, a cat mewing, or a small boy whistling (if he's tuneful), and the story is told of a high school football game being thrown into utter confusion when a mockingbird started to imitate the referee's whistle!

A long, long time ago some kind of mockingbird appeared on what are now known as the Galápagos Islands. Like the Pilgrim Fathers, there were enough of them of both sexes to found a colony. From these early progenitors have evolved four distinct species of Galápagos mockingbirds. Three of them still look like conventional mockingbirds although they differ from the modern mainland kinds in small ways: black ear patches on one, dark breast patches on another, vague streaking on the breasts of all, and absence of the distinctive white wing

Galápagos mockingbird knocking over Darwin finch

"mirrors" of the northern mockingbird. The fourth doesn't even look much like a mocker. It has developed into a lean muscular bird with an outsized, slender, curved beak not unlike that of the long-billed or curve-billed thrashers of the American southwest, and its breast is streak-spotted like a thrasher's.

The strange thing is that, in the absence of shrikes and jays, the Galápagos mockingbirds have turned predatory and a large part of their food is made up of lava lizards, young Darwin finches, and other birds' eggs.

The thrashers, which might better have been called "threshers," are similar in many ways to the mockingbirds and are also accomplished songsters. The brown thrasher, like some people, repeats itself, singing each phrase of its song twice.

Brown thrasher ▶

220

TM Short

Brown Thrasher, ♀
Toxostoma rufum
Pelee Island, L. Erie, Ont.
June 8, 1950

79 Family *Turdidae*
THRUSHES

Some modern systematists relegate the thrushes to subfamily rank within the "catch basin" assemblage known as the Old World flycatchers (*Muscicapidae*). They include, also, the next group, the Old World warblers (including the American gnatcatchers, kinglets, etc.) within that same family. There is some small argument for this; the morphological distinctions between them all are fine but *are* generally recognizable (which is as much as we can say for the family characters of most song birds). To render passé these long-established divisions and a century of literature on what is no more than a heads-or-tails choice, seems at best irresponsible. The most objectionable aspect of the mergers is that they lump together as one unwieldy family more than 1,400 species. The Old World flycatcher family has become the old lady who lived in a shoe.

Just about everybody in urban, suburban, and rural America knows the American robin. Who hasn't seen its struggles with an uncooperative, elastic earthworm under the lawn-sprinkler? Who in the northern regions hasn't been gladdened by its song on chilly mornings before the last snow has melted? But how many know it is a thrush?

In rural areas, both farmer and villager are heartened during the cold March winds by the gentle warble of the returning bluebird. Later they watch fondly as it raises its spot-breasted brood in the hollow top of a fence post. But how many know it is a thrush?

Such unawareness does not exist about the brown, spotted-breasted birds we see in city gardens, parks, ravines, and woodlots as they migrate to their needleleaf evergreen and mixed forest homes. But few know that these are among the very finest of our songsters.

American robin

These are the forest thrushes, the hermit thrush, the Swainson's thrush, and the grey-cheeked thrush (the latter of the far north). They are close relatives, as their musical abilities would suggest, of the Old World nightingale, celebrated in story and song. The nightingale looks just like them except that it lacks spots on its breast in its adult plumage.

From Mexico southward through South America lives another group of forest thrushes, even more like nightingales than the northern thrushes. For obvious reasons, they are called nightingale-thrushes. To this ear, their full songs (not too often heard), are as fine as those of their better known relatives. Unfortunately no poet has listened to their passionate evensongs on a moonlit, tropic night, so they remain obscure to the arts.

80 Family *Sylviidae*
GNATWRENS, GNATCATCHERS, and KINGLETS

From the labyrinth of the roots of an overturned tree, covered with a rank growth of lianas, flows out a *falsetto* whistling trill. If your eyes are sharp you may see a tiny bird, looking like a slender wren. It has a long, narrow bill, and is mostly olive-brown with some buffy and rufous on the cheeks and crown. Its nest is in one of the intertwining clusters of twigs and creepers close to the ground; a dainty, deep cup made of dried grasses, leaf fragments, and soft moss. It is lined with black, hair-like fibres plucked from the bark of the Roseau palm. It is one of the three kinds of gnatwrens found from Mexico and Trinidad to Brazil and Ecuador which are docketed, along with the gnatcatchers and kinglets, among the myriad species of Old World warblers which constitute the family *Sylviidae*.

The gnatcatchers are trim, slender, long-tailed little birds, perhaps as finespun and delicate-looking as any of the avian clan. They are intensely active, almost never still, flitting and fluttering as they go about searching for small insects and spiders. If they should disturb a little moth they skitter after it and catch it, wings beating rapidly and with much ado, for they are not adept flycatchers.

The nests of gnatcatchers are among the most exquisite in bird architecture — as dainty as the builders themselves. Vertically sided little cups fashioned of plant down, they are held together with gossamer bindings of spider web and are usually decorated with lichens of muted greens, blues, and greys and with the petals of small flowers.

224

A young kinglet is among the most appealing of all birds. A tiny ball of soft, fluffy feathers, it has the perkiness of a young puppy. The adult birds retain much of this captivating manner: tame, industrious little minims continually examining leaves and tree-needles for any small creature that might serve as a snack — aphids, insect eggs, tiny moths, grubs.

Black-tailed gnatcatcher

The golden-crowned kinglet's song is a few rising, sibilant notes followed by a gurgly chuckle. The ruby-crowned kinglet, of the same size as the golden-crown, is the little bird with the big voice. Its song starts with a few almost "feeler" notes, high and thin, then swells into a complex warble of some duration, before a finale which is a return to the initial theme, now refined, developed, and elaborated on. The ruby-crown can be distinguished from the golden-crown even at a distance by its mannerism of restlessly twitching its wings like a fidgety fussbudget.

Both kinds of kinglets build large, rounded, purse-like nests with an entrance hole near the top and suspended between several small branches of a coniferous tree.

81 Family *Certhiidae*
TREE CREEPERS

The brown creeper (known as the tree creeper in Britain) is the only one of five distinct species that occurs in the Americas. It is a petite, mouse-like bird of very circumscribed habit. I have seen many hundreds of creepers, both in America and abroad, and, other than on those occasions when I watched them at their nests, I cannot recall a creeper doing anything but just that; hitching its way in short, abrupt advances up the bole of a tree, diligently searching every nook and cranny in the bark for minute insects and spiders and their eggs. When its progress upward reaches the branches, it may continue up a branch or abruptly drop off, and, after a swooping glide that makes it look like a windblown dead leaf, alight near the base of another nearby tree and resume its ascending myopic quest.

In the rare moments when it is *not* doing this, it is only because it pauses long enough to absorb the faint rays of winter sun or else "freezes" until some suspected enemy such as a sharp-shinned hawk passes by.

It even sings from its vertical position on the tree trunk and seldom pauses in its upward clamber to do so. Instead, it throws the song over its shoulder in complete insouciance. Its song is one of the highest-pitched of avian vocalizations (that is, those parts of bird songs that are within the limits of audibility to the human ear; many bird sounds are known only from their presence on sound spectrographs) and can only be approximated by hissing through the front teeth.

The full song, *tsee-tsitsee tseeee-tsizzi*, with many variations, is heard only during late spring and early summer, the birds becoming quite vocal at mating time. Incidentally, mating takes place on a vertical tree-trunk like all other creeper

226

exertions! During winter all one hears from the tiny birds is a whispered *tsss*, the place of origin of which is extremely difficult to trace unless one has seen the bird first. This call note is actually not different from the song but is a mere fragment of it. It is used to communicate with others of its kind and, one suspects, with chickadees and nuthatches and downy woodpeckers; the several species forming a roaming consortium through the bare winter woods.

Brown creeper

The tail feathers of the creeper are stiffened and pointed like those of woodpeckers. So essential are these to its life-style that when the tail feathers are molted, the two central ones remain to furnish the bird with its indispensable prop until the new outer feathers have grown in before they, too, drop out.

In fall and winter, creepers may be found in parks, gardens, and on the now-bare shade trees lining residential streets. They go about their busy business and pay scant attention to human passersby.

Boreal Chickadee ♀
Parus h. hudsonius
Lake St John, P.Q.
Jan. 1954.

T.M.Shortt.

82

Family *Paridae*
TITMICE and CHICKADEES

There are more than sixty species of the bright-eyed, cheerfully active titmice and chickadees in the world, and, being greedy, one wishes there were more. Although thirteen kinds occur in the New World from the tree-limit south to Guatemala, their absence from Honduras southward through South America is missed.

These busy, small birds look upon humans as being simply a perambulatory part of their environment. If they learn to associate you with a handout of food (a relationship that is easily achieved), they will alight on you and search your clothing, even going into pockets. But — a warning — if they don't find anything after becoming accustomed to a windfall of tidbits, they will scold you in no uncertain terms. On occasion I've been convinced that chickadees can swear!

Our most familiar member of the group is the black-capped chickadee which has gained immense popularity by its regular, winter-long visits to urban and suburban bird feeding stations erected in gardens, on porches, or even on apartment balconies and window sills. Its clear whistled call, *chick-a-dee-dee*, from which it gets its name, is an optimistic sound even in the darkest days of winter.

In the vast needleleaf evergreen forests of northern Canada we find the boreal chickadee, a fluffy, brown-capped species. It sounds like a black-capped with a head cold (or a little tipsy), its call being a more lethargic, *tzick-ah-dzey-dzey*.

◀ *Boreal chickadee*

83 Family *Sittidae*
NUTHATCHES

The name *Sittidae* comes from the Greek word for a nuthatch, *sitte*. The etymology of "nuthatch" is a little more conjectural. It was no doubt gained from the birds' habit of wedging nuts and hard-covered seeds into cracks and crannies of tree bark and hammering away with the chisel-like bill until the shell is riven. Originally it probably was "nuthack" (hack from the German *hacke*, a mattock, which was a sort of pick, double-bitted with an adze on one end and a chisel on the other).

Having decided, then, that these are "nutpickers," let us watch one as it starts its food search high up on a big branch of a tree. The first thing we notice is that it is upside down, clinging with its outsized feet, one of which is directed outwards and backwards from the body. It literally hangs by this foot and supports itself with the other. Now, head foremost, it commences to climb down the bark (among birds an ability exclusive to the nuthatches). As it works its jerky way down, with the strong, sharp claws gripping the ridges of bark, every furrow and crease of the bark is closely scrutinized for spiders, small insects and their larvae and eggs. Every so often it gives a sidling, sideways lurch as it changes the backward-clinging foot from right to left. When near the base of the tree trunk, it leaves that tree and flies strongly to the upper branches of another, where, again upside down, it repeats the downward climb. As it comes closer, we see that it does not use its tail (which is soft and short) for support as the woodpeckers, woodcreepers, and tree creepers do.

The brown-headed nuthatch of the open pine forests of
the southeastern United States occasionally uses a flake of pine
bark, held firmly in the bill, to wedge and prise off other loose
bits of bark that it is unable to dislodge with its bill. This is a

Brown-headed nuthatch

primitive form of "tool-using," rare among birds and indeed
even among mammals. Other notable avian tool-users are the
celebrated Darwin finches of the genus *Cactospiza*, and the
Egyptian vulture, which "throws" stones with its beak at
ostrich eggs until it breaks them open. The use of a piece of
bark by the regent bower bird and a clump of leaves by the
satin bower bird as paint brushes to apply a mixture of
charcoal, fruit juice, and saliva to their bowers, are other
examples. And it might be considered that birds such as
woodpeckers and nuthatches, which force acorns and other
nuts into bark fissures and peck them until they split, are using
a form of clamp and anvil.

84 BUNTINGS

Family *Emberizidae;* subfamily *Emberizinae*

This group of about 160 species is mostly confined to the Americas, but about three dozen kinds have "colonized" the Old World; most are now distinct species; for example the corn bunting, yellowhammer, reed bunting, ortolan. The snow bunting and the Lapland longspur have remained conspecific with their North American populations. Most of the buntings are of the size of a "sparrow," hence the American name for many members of the family: song sparrow, white-throated sparrow, Andean sparrow, fox sparrow. For the most part they are open-country or ground-inhabiting birds with strong legs and feet. The bill approaches, among birds, nearest the ideal cone, combining the strength to crush seeds with the delicacy of touch to pick up small objects such as insects.

A characteristic of this family and the *Fringillidae*, from which they are doubtfully separated, is the angulation of the mouth. The beak opening runs in almost a straight line from the tip until near the base where it turns abruptly down. These merry little birds, then, are nonetheless "down in the mouth"!

I prefer to include in the *Emberizidae* the Darwin finches, subfamily *Geospizinae*, of the Galápagos Islands even though some recent revisions place them with the essentially Old World family *Fringillidae*. It seems likely that they had their origin in an early Central American fauna — perhaps from a common ancestor of birds like the towhees or saltators. The thirteen distinct Galápagos species (another is found on Cocos Island) are those birds of diverse habit (and hence striking modifications of the bill) that convinced Charles Darwin of the

Darwin finches ▶

232

Camarhynchus parvulus ♂
May 18, 1965
Academy Bay, Santa Cruz I.
Galápagos

Small Insectivorous Tree Finch

T.M.Shortt

Platyspiza crassirostris ♂
Academy bay, Santa Cruz I.
Galápagos
May 17, 1965.

Vegetarian Tree Finch

T.M.Shortt

Large Insectivorous Tree Finch ♂
Camarhynchus psittaculus.
Isla Santa Cruz,
Galápagos
May 19 1965

T.M.Shortt

Warbler Finch ♂
Certhidea olivacea
Academy bay, Santa Cruz I.
Galápagos
May 18, 1965

T.M.Shortt

reality of adaptive radiation — the proliferation of new forms from one source through genetic experimentation combined with environmental opportunities. The great diversity that has resulted from their evolutionary history has provided one with the beak of a warbler, one with the beak of a grosbeak, one with a long, strong, fruit-eating beak that is also suitable for probing into cactus flowers. Some are insectivorous, some granivorous, with beaks of varying size and stoutness for crushing seeds of all degrees of size and hardness, and, most remarkable of all, two are tool-users.

"El Senor sparrow"
(Andean Sparrow)

One, the woodpecker finch, uses a small twig or spine to flush out or actually impale grubs living in wood or bark too hard for the bird to chip away with its beak. The use of a probe or "toothpick" is not an exception but rather a normal procedure. The first woodpecker finch that I saw was engaged in just such an exploit and was using the spine from a pad of the *Opuntia Echios*, the prickly-pear cactus tree of Santa Cruz Island. I know this, for the finch, having secured its prey, dropped its pick, which whirled down on to my outstretched palm.

234

Family *Emberizidae;* subfamily *Cardinalinae*
85 CARDINAL GROSBEAKS

This is a strictly American branch of the huge emberizine family. It is made up of about 110 species, of which the majority live in Central and South America. As well as the familiar bird that gives the group its name — the red cardinal, with its high, expressive, cardinal-red crest and black face — and its more soberly colored South American relatives, this division also contains the blue, rose-breasted, black-headed, and yellow grosbeaks, and a number of related tropical forms: the strange parrot-billed pyrrhuloxia of the southwestern United States, the brilliantly colored *Passerina* buntings, the seed-eaters, grassquits, brush-finches, and others.

The name "cardinal," of course, comes from its red color — an ecclesiastical cardinal's hat; but *his* name comes from the Latin *cardinalis* which means "that upon which something hinges or depends," hence important, principal, as the cardinal point; *that*, in turn, comes from *cardo*, a door-hinge. So, in the final analysis, the cardinal was named after door hardware!

The red cardinal ranges over most of the United States south to Belize and Guatemala and has greatly extended its range northward in the last century.

The American buntings are small birds which excite our admiration because of the brilliant colors of the males. Best known is the indigo bunting, an intense indigo-blue, which is constant on the head and shot with glancing greenish highlights on the body. Equally gorgeous is the painted bunting, with rich blue head, golden-green back, and underparts of intense vermilion; the lazuli bunting with head and neck azure-blue and underparts orange-chestnut changing to white on the belly; the rich, dark blue Mexican blue bunting; Rosita's bunting, bright blue except for the lower breast which is rosy-red; and the strangely colored varied bunting which looks all black until viewed in direct sunlight when it is seen to be the color of fine claret with various patches of scarlet and blue. It is aptly named *Passerina versicolor*—*versicolor* meaning "I turn various colors."

Lazuli bunting

The birds that comprise the complex of seed-eaters, pygmy finches, grassquits, and seed-finches are tiny. The many species are abundant in Central and South America, living in savannas, open brushy country, pastures, weedy edges, and semi-clearings in forests. The little blue-black grassquit often nests in loose colonies in cane or rice fields.

Cardinal ▶

Cardinal. ♂
(Richmondena c. cardenales)

Point Pelee, Ontario

May 15 1941

TMShortt

86 HONEYCREEPERS

Family *Emberizidae;* subfamily *Coerebinae*

Until recently the honeycreepers were recognized as a separate
family made up of about thirty-five species of birds which had
as a unifying feature a deeply bifid, penicillate tongue — that
is, two-lobed and ending in a brush-like tip — an
accommodation for feeding on the nectar of flowers.

Recent revisions have wrought havoc with this group.
Some include all of them with the tanagers which, in turn, are
dumped into the already bulging conglomerate called
Emberizidae. Others lift most of them and place them with the
tanagers but locate about ten with the wood warblers (some of
which have penicillate tongues). Still others temporize by
setting them up as a "tribe" nearest to, but outside, that group.
Thus things are illuminated and clarified until they are dim
and opaque.

Since the main function of all systems of nomenclature is
to provide simplicity and intelligibility of communication, it
seems best to consider them as a two-pronged unit, of
subfamily rank, within the catch-all of the *Emberizidae*. It
would appear that collectively they represent a miscellaneous
assemblage of birds, now united by convergent evolution into
brush-tongued nectar-eaters.

The best known of the honeycreepers is the bananaquit,
found throughout the West Indies, southern Mexico, and
south to Argentina. It is one of those species that for some
reason has adapted to the human presence and may be found
about dwellings, ornamental trees, flower gardens, and

plantations. Contrary to its name, it is not especially fond of bananas but does some fortuitous damage to them in scrabbling around with its sharp, scratchy claws over young growing fruit which, when mature, bear raised dark scars from the lesions. It is fond of sapadillos but its main diet is the nectar from flowers and incidental small insects which have also been attracted to the honey.

Green honeycreeper

The green honeycreeper is typical of a large group in which the males are brightly colored in strong, harsh, often discordant colors (for example, purple-blue and bright blue-green together!) mostly purples, deep blues, and parrot-greens. Their longish bills are sharply pointed and somewhat downcurved, suited for insertion into tubular flowers.

The flower-piercers have curious beaks, slightly upturned and furnished with a shrike-like, sharply hooked tip with which they cut or "bite" holes through the corolla of tubular blossoms to get at the nectary. These kinds of nectar-eaters probably are of little value as pollinators, bypassing as they do the pollen-bearing anthers. Most of the probing species perform this useful function.

Family *Emberizidae;* subfamily *Thraupinae*
87 TANAGERS

The Tupi Indians of Brazil called these brilliantly colored birds *tangara*. An early taxonomist, naming one of them, assigned to it a generic title based on this barbarous name, but somewhere along the line a transposition of letters took place (a typesetter's error perhaps) and it appeared instead, as *Tanagra*. From this perversity, the English name "tanager" has evolved. Rightfully they should be called "tangaras," not tanagers. But tanagers they are and will so remain. But their affinities, to the wood warblers and honeycreepers on the one hand and to the buntings and sparrows on the other, are still uncertain. At the time when only the North American forms had been studied, the presence of a notch or "tooth" on the cutting edge of the upper mandible served as a distinctive character; but many of the tropical forms lack this obvious feature. It is not nature's way to conform to a rigid system which places blocks of species in neatly circumscribed compartments, and no linear system that can possibly be devised will ever adequately demonstrate the complexities of avian interrelationships.

The tanagers, made up of some two hundred distinct species, are almost entirely tropical American. Four species — the scarlet, western, summer, and hepatic tanagers — have pioneered northward into the temperate parts of North America. Conversely, a few occur southward to central Argentina including the lovely white-capped tanager — entirely deep cornflower-blue with a cap of silvery white feathers on the crown. Some species penetrate the dense

Blue tanager ▶

240

~TMSholl

Blue Tanager ♂
Thraupis episcopus
Maracas Valley. Trinidad
May 1957

evergreen rain forests but most are birds of the leafy, airy crowns of lighter woods and so are not difficult to observe.

The familiar northern tanagers are among the larger members of the group (seven to eight inches); most of the tropical species are smaller and display a bewildering variety of attractive, bright, color combinations. The paradise tanager of Colombia to Brazil exhibits every one of the spectrum colors in one part of its plumage or another.

Blue-necked tanager

The naturalist who sees for the first time a blue tanager is invariably awed, for instead of the strong, multicolored plumage typical of tanagers, this bird is entirely a light, ethereal blue not unlike the mountain bluebird of western North America. It seems totally out of place in its robust tropical surroundings — as if a small fragment of the heavens had drifted down, or as if a wisp of smoke had gained corporeality.

242

88 SWALLOW-TANAGER

Family *Emberizidae;* subfamily *Tersininae*

Swallow-Tanager

Formerly given full family rank as *Tersinidae*, the swallow-tanager has recently been reduced to a subfamily although some authors still consider that the aberrant tanager- and swallow-like bird deserves full recognition as a separate family. At any rate, it still perches out on its own twig on a branch of the evolutionary tree. The size of the twig makes little difference.

Perched, it looks like a tanager but when it opens its long, pointed wings and flies, the resemblance to a graceful, rapidly flying swallow becomes apparent. The beak is short, very broad, and depressed, not unlike that of a purple martin but more turgid. The sexes are quite unalike: the male is all-over

243

bright turquoise-blue, the feathers having a hard, glossy surface as if enameled — which results in glinting highlights of cerulean and green. The face, wing-tips, and short bars on the flanks are black and the belly is white; altogether a very handsome bird. The female, if somewhat duller, is colorful enough to be mistaken as a male of a second species (it has been). The general color of the upper parts and of the chest is bright grass-green, the throat and face are dark brown, and the lower breast and belly light yellow with spearshaped dark brown markings.

The swallow-tanager ranges from Panama and Trinidad south to Argentina, Paraguay, Bolivia, and Peru. It prefers high country during the nesting season and, in Trinidad, may be found in the higher reaches of the Northern Range on Morne Bleu, Mount Aripo, and Mount El Tucuche where it nests in tunnels which the female digs into earthen banks. In some parts of their range they nest in crevices of rock cliffs, in crannies on buildings, and even in hollow trees. Any sort of cul-de-sac or blind alley will do. After the nesting season swallow-tanagers descend to lower altitudes and sometimes may be seen in flocks about open woodlands; a score or more often perch in the topmost branches of a dead tree from which vantage point they hawk for insects like swallow-shaped flycatchers.

One of the peculiarities of the swallow-tanager is the resilient skin of its throat which is distendable into a sort of pouch. This often becomes hideously misshapen as the bird stuffs it with berries and other fruits. It cannot be said to have what we would call a song, but it monotonously utters shrill, unmusical notes of a clinking metallic quality.

Swallow-tanager ▶

Tersina viridis
Swallow-Tanager ♂
Morne Bleu, Trinidad
June 1957

TMShort

89 WOOD WARBLERS

Family *Parulidae*

The name "wood warbler," although serviceable, is not eminently suitable for this family of about 110 species. While many are woodland birds, others are dwellers of fresh and saltwater marches, swamps, the shrubbery of semi-desert, coastal mangrove, and dry second growth; and the term "warbler" carries implications of a non-existent relationship to the Old World warbler family — never mind that very few of them can be said, by any interpretation, to warble.

Although outnumbered by some other families in kinds, the wood warblers must rank near the top in numbers of individuals in North America. They are also common enough in Central and South America. Nearly every type of woodland habitat, in addition to the non-sylvan biospheres mentioned above — from the stunted, scattered spruce and hemlock at the northern limits of trees to the epiphyte-laden cloud forests of the tropics — is occupied by one or more species of wood warbler.

All are small birds, few of them reaching more than five inches in total length. Yellow is the predominant bright color, usually in combination with muted blue or greenish upperparts (slaty and olivaceous shades) and marked with black or chestnut streaks or spots. Some exhibit areas of orange; tropical species often display patches of red. One species, the singularly beautiful red warbler of the pine forests of the high Mexican plateau, is entirely red except for a silvery cheek patch which has a silken sheen.

246

The wood warblers of the north are highly migratory and provide, in the spring, one of the feature events of the bird-watching year. A day's list may be creditably swelled by the tabulation of a dozen or more easily and quickly identified kinds. The scene changes in the fall as the dull-colored immatures and adults in vaguely marked autumn and winter plumage pour southward. Many an hour has been lost in exasperating and vain attempts to identify fall warblers. No such problem exists in the tropics, for, with few exceptions, male and female wood warblers of the warmer regions are alike in dress and there is no seasonal change of plumage.

Red warbler

One species, Kirtland's warbler, is one of the rarest of birds with a severely circumscribed range. It nests only in Michigan in young jackpines in an area of less than eighty miles in diameter. Twice annually, the few hundred individuals face a long and hazardous migration to and from their Bahama Islands wintering grounds, besides the additional threat of being one of the species most commonly victimized by the brood-parasitic cowbird.

Yellow-headed Blackbird. ♂
(*Xanthocephalus xanthocephalus*)
Devil's Creek, Selkirk, Manitoba.
Aug. 2 1930

T.M.Shortt

90 Family *Icteridae*
ICTERIDS

This heterogeneous group of about ninety species of New World birds is so diverse and its component segments have so many long-established and erroneous names, that it is difficult to select one convenient, comprehensive title for all of them. Ornithologists use the term "icterids." We may find this a strange family name to apply to such familiar birds as the meadowlark, Baltimore oriole, grackle, cowbird, and bobolink, but since none of these names is in any way all-inclusive, icterids it must be and we may as well get used to it.

All icterids are sturdy birds ranging in size from six to twenty-one inches; their bills are hard, conical, and pointed, and the gape lacks rictal bristles; the feet are large and strong. With these rather vague generalizations about their morphology, we leave the beginner on his own.

The birds themselves have divided into a number of very different groups that have occupied just about every major terrestrial and arboreal niche in the Americas; each group is made up of showy, noisy, and easily observed forms so the amateur has little trouble getting to know them. He may find it harder to assimilate the fact that they — the red-winged blackbird, meadowlark, bobolink, etc. — are all icterids. And that matters little.

A name sometimes given to the group is "hangnests," fitting enough for the orioles, troupials, and their large tropical relatives, the caciques and oropendolas, but hardly suitable for the ground-nesting meadowlarks, bobolinks, and military

◄ *Yellow-headed blackbird*

blackbirds — and certainly not for the cowbirds, most of which make no nest at all but pop their eggs into those of other birds!

The skillful weaving of the bag-like, pensile nests of the orioles and hangnests constitutes one of the marvels of avian

Oropendola

architecture. This reaches its highest achievement in the colony nesting yellowtails and oropendolas. The nests of these birds may reach a length of five or even six feet; great pendant pouches, dozens of which may hang from a single giant tree. One of these colonies is an intensely active place, the action accompanied by much noise. The delivery of the "songs" of these birds is not accomplished without great effort. The male makes a profound bow, bringing his head below the level of his perch and raising the tail to vertical or beyond. The song is made up of gurgling sounds with simultaneous squeaks and squeals like a rusty wagonwheel in motion, plunks like huge, falling drops of water, whistles, and even strange crashing sounds. Both the song and accompanying antics are astonishing.

91 PEPPERSHRIKES

The peppershrikes, of which there are only two species, are chunky birds possessing strong heavy bills, hooked at the tip like those of the true shrikes. They live in the middle storeys of more or less open forest or in the brushy margins and about clearings in heavier rain forest. They range from eastern and southern Mexico south to the northern parts of Argentina. They are, for their size of about six inches, rather slow-moving, sluggishly deliberate birds but are capable of short bursts of activity — as when pursuing a cicada, mantis, or other large insect (they seem not to bother much with smaller insects). When a peppershrike has captured one of these or a large beetle, it holds it down with its strong feet and proceeds to peck it and tear it to pieces with its bird-of-prey beak. When a cicada is being thus dismantled it sets up a loud buzzing noise as its tymballs (oval, ribbed sound-making structures) buckle and vibrate in protest. This stridence, in concert with the slaps and thumps being administered to the hard chitinous exoskeleton of the insect by the even harder, horny beak of the peppershrike, engenders a small bedlam. Like a family quarrel on a suburban street it brings out all the neighbors to see what is going on. Tanagers, wood warblers, wrens, honeycreepers, and other birds flit about with some vague concern at the violence being enacted near their homes.

The song of the rufous-browed peppershrike is a clear, pleasing, whistled warble with something of the timbre of the song of the solitary vireo. If one listens closely enough, he will hear that it asks an impudent question: the song has been

Rufous-browed Peppershrike
Cyclarhis gujanensis ♂
nr Curepe, Trinidad
May 14, 1957

TWShort

paraphrased as "D'you *wash* ev'ry *week*?" and, as if expecting an answer, follows with "I'm *wait*ing to *hear* you."

The irises of the eyes of peppershrikes are an odd shade of orange-brown. They are rimmed with naked eyelids of a rather

Rufous-browed peppershrike

inflamed pink. Somehow one gets the impression (quite erroneous) that it has weak eyes. They look like the eyes of a person who has worn eyeglasses constantly for many years and has just removed them. They look as though they smarted a little.

Peppershrikes build shallow, suspended nests somewhat like those of vireos but more fragile.

◀ *Rufous-browed peppershrike*

92 Family *Vireonidae*
VIREOS and GREENLETS

The forty-odd species in this exclusively New World family form an extremely uniform series of birds of about four to a little more than six inches in length, most of them largely grey-green in color, sometimes with slaty or yellow areas, but none brightly colored. The name *vireo* is Latin and means "I am green" or "I am flourishing"; its reference obviously being to the healthy green of plant foliage, which leads us to opine that if the leaves of our houseplants took on a vireo-green shade we would hasten to supply some plant food packed with nitrogen and phosphoric acid.

The vireos are incessant singers. When most if not all other birds have become quiet in the heat of midday, the vireos sing on. Their simple arias, often in a sweet voice, are repetitive and unemotional, hence monotonous. In a lounge-chair under the shade of a tree in my garden on a midsummer's day, I have been driven nearly to distraction by a red-eyed vireo up in that same shade tree, whose two or three-syllable phrases, each with a pause of equal length in between, some rising, some falling like questions and answers, persevered until well into the cool of evening. Not for nothing did New Englanders dub it "the preacher-bird."

One species is named the Philadelphia vireo, *Vireo philadelphicus* (it breeds mostly in the northern coniferous forest belt in mixed poplar-spruce-birch lands); *phileo*, I love and *delphicus*, a brother, (the brotherly-love vireo?) Its song is something like that of the red-eye but with exasperatingly long pauses between phrases. Just when you think it has stopped singing or has flown away, it sings again.

254

The greenlets are a tropical group of vireos, smaller and with proportionately longer and more slender bills. They are common birds of scrub and forest, from lowland mangrove swamps, bamboo clumps, cocoa plantations, and open woodland up to the cloud forests. They are occasionally seen in small parties often in company with warblers (which they resemble in their actions) and other small forest birds. Their

Slaty-capped shrike vireo

sociability is at variance with the behavior of the larger vireos. Greenlets are maddeningly difficult to identify as to species. They lack almost all markings that might be distinctive and vary from each other only in relative *shades* of color.

The three species of shrike vireos are sometimes given separate family rank. Those who have heard their harsh, scolding cries and persistent, monotonous songs will suspect that they belong in the *Vireonidae*. They are strikingly marked birds: the slaty-capped shrike vireo is greenish above with a slate-blue head, yellow superciliary (eyebrow) stripe and throat, and bright pink feet.

TMShortt

Blue Jay ♂
Cyanocitta cristata
Toronto, Ontario
Dec. 1966

93 Family *Corvidae*
CROWS and JAYS

The *Corvidae*, which embrace about a hundred different
species, are divided into two well-marked subfamilies: the
Corvinae, crows, ravens, nutcrackers, choughs, and the smaller
more colorful *Garrulinae*, the jays, magpies, tree pies. They
have successfully learned to live and even to thrive in the
"manscape," in fact to such an extent that some ornithologists
say they are the most intelligent of birds. Certainly controlled
experiments have indicated that the crows possess good
capacity for learning.

That they flourish in country radically changed by man's
activities can be attributed, in part, to intelligence, for they are
bold and sagacious, but in greater measure to the fact that they
are omnivores — they will eat and thrive on anything, animal
or vegetable, that is edible.

Some individuals find a good living on garbage dumps; all
of them like sprouting grain; eggs and young birds are eagerly
consumed in season; some turn beachcomber and exist on
dead fish and other refuse that washes ashore. They are among
the most highly adaptable of birds, yet in their all-embracing
dietary habit and almost world-wide range, the corvids have
not appreciably changed in either form or color.

All of the thirty-odd species are almost of a size and all are
black, black with grey cape and belly, or black with white cape
and belly. The big all-black northern raven is the largest; in
fact, it is the largest of the passerine song birds.

The jays are almost as prosperous as the crows but have
undergone considerable amendment of color, ornamentation

◀ *Blue jay*

257

(long tails in some kinds and a variety of crests, some of them bizarre), and habit. They have become more specialized ecologically. Some are desert-dwellers, some inhabit the northern coniferous forests, others live in semi-arid lowlands, in dense wooded areas in mountain gullies, in mangrove swamps, brushy cattle country, thorn forests, high pine-oak woods, and even humid cloud forests. Most are rather severely restricted, each to its own habitat.

American crow

The majority of New World jays are blue or partly blue, the tonal range being from the deep almost black blue of the Steller's jay and many of the Mexican jays, through the bright shades of the blue jay and the turquoise jay of the Andes, to the more delicate azure hues of the crestless jays of the genus *Aphelocoma*. Exceptions to the general blueness of jays are the grey jay or whisky Jack of the northern evergreen forests, the big robust brown jay of the Mexican scrub and humid lowlands, and the beautiful green jay which ranges from southern Texas to Honduras and again from Venezuela to Bolivia.

94 OLD WORLD FINCHES

Family *Fringillidae;* subfamily *Carduelinae*

In the latest revisions of avian classification, this family which once included all of the New World emberizine sparrows, cardinals, and buntings has now been much restricted. The recognition of two centers of origin and distribution of these conical-billed seed-eating birds is the basis for separating the essentially western hemisphere groups from those of the eastern. This does not mean that all kinds now occurring in either of the two hemispheres necessarily originated there. About thirty-six American emberizine buntings colonized Europe and Asia and penetrated Africa; conversely, some twenty-five species of Old World finches have infiltrated America. These include the purple and house finches, pine and evening grosbeaks, the redpolls and goldfinches, and the crossbills. All are found more or less throughout the northern hemisphere, represented in the Old World by identical or closely related species.

Seed-bearing plants are, geologically speaking, of recent origin. They only became dominant plant forms as late as the Miocene epoch (ten to twenty-five million years ago) and we can assume that all of the seed-eaters evolved during and after that time; insect-eaters had already existed for millions of years.

The *Fringillidae* are divided into two groups—the *Fringillinae* and the *Carduelinae*. The *Fringillinae* consist only of the brambling and the chaffinches which have no crop and finer, thinner bills; the *Carduelinae* embrace sixty-eight species, most northern in distribution but with strong representation in Africa.

259

The majority live in the needleleaf evergreen forests, and it is these kinds that have penetrated into the Americas. They are found wherever coniferous trees grow, down the North American West Coast, along the great Mexican plateau, and even beyond. Siskins and goldfinches have infiltrated South America as far as the Straits of Magellan.

White-winged crossbill

The most remarkable members of the family are the crossbills. They have the beak curiously modified for efficient extraction of seeds from cones. The curved upper and lower mandibles cross like the blades of scissors. When opened they act like prying wedges which spread the scales of the cone wide apart; the bird's tongue then deftly extracts the nourishing kernel.

Pine grosbeak ▶

Pine Grosbeak ♂
(Pinicola e. leucura)
Fort Albany, Ont.
June 20, 1942.

T M Shortt

GLOSSARY

amphoric   Sound produced by blowing across small mouth of a large vessel (Amphora, Greek or Roman vase).

bifid   Deeply cleft into two lobes.

bromeliad   Member of a plant family of the American tropics (*Bromeliaciae*), most of them epiphytes — "perching plants."

cancellated   Formed of interlacing fibres and plates, porous.

conspecific   Of the same kind; one species.

concatentater   One who links together, "lumper."

concentric   Having a common center, e.g. concentric ripples caused by an object striking calm water surface.

crepuscular   Active in half-light, especially twilight.

cursorial   Adapted for running.

decurved   Curved downward.

diurnal   Active during the daytime; not nocturnal.

emberizine   Of the family *Emberizidae*.

dorso-ventrally   From back to front.

epiphytes   Non-parasitic air-plants growing on tree limbs; not rooted in the ground; usually orchids, ferns, bromeliads.

gallinaceous   A term applied to fowl-like birds; pheasants, quail, partridges, grouse, guineafowl, turkeys, etc., of the order *galliformes*.

gape   The part of the beak that opens; the mouth.

granivorous   Grain-eating.

262

gular pouch   L. *gula*, throat, hence throat pouch; in birds often extending beneath the beak between the rami (extended prongs of the jawbone which meet in front and form lower section of the beak).

hybrid   Offspring, the result of the mating of two different species, usually sterile.

imbricate   Angle and arrangement of the insertion of feathers into the skin, determining overlap.

incurvate   Bent into a curve, curved down and inwards, not raised; curled inwards from both sides towards center.

inosculating   Interweaving circles.

inspissated   Congealed; hardened.

integument   Skin or other natural covering.

interstitial   Forming spaces.

intumescent   Swollen. In ornithology without the inference of morbidity.

iris   Flat, circular, colored membrane surrounding the pupil of the eye.

liana   Climbing plants of the tropical forest, many of them with woody stems. A general term like "tree," not specific.

lobate   Equipped with lobes; with flattish projecting parts.

mandible   Upper or lower part of bird's beak.

morphology   Physical form of animals or plants.

natatorial   Of swimming.

Neotropical   Literally new tropical; that is tropical America (the New World).

panache   Tuft of feathers used as a head-dress, especially on a hat or helmet.

pectination   Comb-like structure; toothed fringe.

piscivorous   Fish-eating.

precocious or precocial   Of young birds that hatch clothed and are able to run about or swim almost immediately. Opposite: altricial; hatched naked, blind and helpless.

prehensile   Capable of taking hold; grasping.

omnivorous   Feeding on anything edible.

operculum   Lid-like valve covering an aperture.

pied   Piebald; of two colors arranged in large patches; especially black and white, e.g. magpie.

pterylography   The description of the arrangement of feathers on a bird's body; feathered tracts and unfeathered spaces. The arrangement is different in different families.

raptorial   Preying on other animals.

recurved   Curving upward.

rugose   Naturally rough or wrinkled.

sac   Bag-like membranous cavity in animal organism.

subcutaneous   Under the skin.

superciliary   Above the eye, eyebrow.

syrinx   The lower larynx, the voice-organ of birds; the song-organ.

taxonomy   Principles of classification; arrangement of plants, animals in orderly, logical sequence.

transpiration   Exhalation of watery vapor.

truncated   Ending abruptly, as if cut off at the tip.

tubercles   Wart-like outgrowths, but natural, not abnormal.

wattles   Fleshy appendages, usually on head or throat, usually pendulous.

INDEX TO COLOR PLATES

INDEX TO ILLUSTRATIONS

INDEX

271

Black-necked stilt